If This is a Man

Primo Levi
If This is a Man

Translated by Stuart Woolf

*With an Introduction by Frederic Raphael
and an Afterword by the author*

Etchings by Jane Joseph

LONDON
The Folio Society
2000

Se questo è un uomo was first published in Italy in 1947. This edition follows the translation first published by The Orion Press in 1960, with minor emendations.

This edition published by The Folio Society Ltd
44 Eagle Street, London WC1R 4FS
www.foliosociety.com

This edition published by arrangement with The Random House Group Ltd and Viking Penguin, a division of Penguin Putnam Inc.

Typeset at The Folio Society in Minion with Helvetica display. Printed on Lessebo paper by TJ International, Padstow, and bound by them in cloth blocked and printed with a design by the artist

Eighth printing 2009

Contents

Illustrations

8   Illustrations

Introduction

In some respects, Primo Levi needs no introduction. His work has become a classic requiring neither commentary nor explanation. If the style is the man, one might imagine, from its tone and vocabulary, that its author was someone of unassuming appearance and manner. He once said that he modelled his account of life in Auschwitz (or more precisely in Monowitz-Buna, an adjacent *Arbeitslager* or 'work-camp') on 'the weekly report commonly used in factories'. His intention was to write in a language accessible to all. It does not follow that he, personally, was as guileless as his forthright and unadorned narrative. His plain speaking was calculated to give the world no excuse not to follow every word of what he had to say.

Behind his truthful modesty, which led him to describe his companions more thoroughly than himself, Primo (as his biographer, Myriam Anissimov, like his other admirers, impels us to call him) was able to control, although not to hide, his abiding sense of outrage and scandal: Auschwitz, in his view, changed inexorably any assumptions that civilised man might have concerning himself or his God. Primo's candour was as undeceived about himself as it was about others. While he gives the impression of a reasonable man of science ambushed by the monsters of unreason, he was as astute as he contrived to seem artless. If he insisted that chance alone enabled him to survive the camps, it is clear that, in the small areas where it was possible, Levi knew how to make, or at least to improve, his own luck. His survival might be due to chance, but he was never close to becoming a '*Muselmann*', the term given to those spectral inmates of the camps who, by their listlessness, showed that they had renounced all prospect of survival. Levi was a lover of Dante who refused to abandon hope merely because he had stepped through the gates of hell.

Primo was born in Turin, on 31 July 1919, in the large family apartment where he was to live all his life, save for the time he spent first in the mountains, as a member of a partisan group, and then at Auschwitz, and finally on the perilous journey home which he described in *La Tregua* (*The Truce*). Family tradition says that his birth took place in the room which would later be his study. His ancestors were Sephardic Jews, refugees from the Spanish Inquisition. Their descendants had been in Italy for more than three and a half centuries when Mussolini, under pressure from Hitler, declared them to be aliens and outcasts.

Italian Jews had been, in many respects, the most assimilated in Europe. If they had to endure the usual taunts from Christian schoolfellows, they were rarely victims of systematic discrimination. Before (and often after) the Risorgimento, which unified the country only in 1861, most Italians felt more allegiance to their native cities than to the nation. The Jews' undivided enthusiasm made them, in many ways, exemplary citizens of the new state. Italy had unlocked the gates of the ghetto which, for as long as Rome was still ruled by the Popes, literally enclosed the 'perfidious Jews' (as they were described in Catholic doctrine until Vatican II rescinded the anathema).

Jews were not, at first, always hostile to the 'anti-Communist' movement which Benito Mussolini founded in the year of Primo's birth. Alexander Stille's *Benevolence and Betrayal* gives memorable accounts of the varying attitudes, and fates, of five Italian Jewish families under Fascism. Not a few continued to be blindly loyal to the Duce even when, in 1938, he betrayed them by promulgating racist laws copied from the Nazis whose barbarity he had earlier derided.

Even those Jews who were disgusted – as was Primo's father – by the vulgarity of the Fascist parades and speeches had found it almost impossible not to acquiesce in the dominant political and social climate. As Dan Vittorio Segre remarks, in his *Memoirs of a Fortunate Jew*, Fascism became 'the only natural form of existence' for Italians during the inter-war years. When Mussolini unwisely opted for alliance with Germany, patriotism demanded acquiescence or silence.

It is tempting to depict Primo as growing up as an unworldly science student, of a nervous disposition, who was caught up only by mischance in the hellish machinery of Hitler's war against the Jews. To some extent he fostered this reluctant vision of himself. In fact, although addictively bookish, he was a surprisingly active and decisive young man. If timid with women, he was an amusing companion. As far as politics were concerned, he was indisposed to fatalism and capable of brave, even reckless decisions. Although of unimpressive physique (thin and fair-haired), he learned to be a resolute mountaineer in the company of his close friends, Jewish and Gentile, who were decidedly anti-Fascist, though never Communist.

Primo's father, Cesare, had observed, and been horrified by, Béla Kun's 1919 revolutionary government in Hungary, which he had visited while working as an electrical engineer. He always feared that Jews would attract persecution by becoming identified with Bolshevism. Primo was to remain wary of ideologies, as of metaphysics, but he was soon drawn to the movement *Giustizia e Libertà* ('Justice and Liberty'), which had been founded by Carlo Rosselli in 1928. Ten years later, Carlo and his brother were to be murdered in France, in an incident which prompted Alberto

Moravia to write *Il Conformista*, later the basis for a film directed by Bernardo Bertolucci which convincingly reconstructs the moral and social vacuousness of Italian Fascism.

Primo dated the criminal insolence of Fascism from an earlier murder, that of the socialist deputy Giuseppe Matteotti, who was done to death in 1924 on Mussolini's orders. The brazenness with which the Duce denied responsibility, and the facility with which his lies prevailed, were echoed even more savagely by Adolf Hitler, ten years later, on the so-called 'Night of the Long Knives', when he ordered the murders of a number of his enemies, and more of his one-time friends. Europe had entered a time of consciencelessness from which, as Primo was to discover, it proved unwilling to wake. The phenomenon of 'Holocaust denial', whose authors claim that the gas chambers were a figment of Zionist propaganda, is of a piece with the Fascist dictators' refusal to take responsibility for their crimes, or to see them as criminal. Primo Levi's later years were bedevilled by the fear that, for all the clarity and honesty of his narrative, his evidence had not been believed.

If, as a socialist group, *Giustizia e Libertà* was not avowedly extremist, its partisans did not flinch from extreme means. There were sporadic, sometimes spectacular, acts of defiance: for instance, the dropping of leaflets over Milan in 1930. Most of their plans, however, proved as abortive as the plot to assassinate Mussolini. By the late 1930s, nearly all of the leaders of the movement had been arrested. Only those in Turin, led by Carlo Levi (the author of *Christ Stopped at Eboli*), avoided detection for a while. Hence Primo's native city became, by elimination, the centre of anti-Fascist intellectual activity. The philosopher Benedetto Croce, who had recanted from his early endorsement of the Duce, was its inspiration.

The outbreak of war brought about no immediate or marked

change in Primo's life. The anti-Jewish laws did not yet impinge cruelly on a community which somewhat gloried in its now hermetic separateness. Unlike in Germany, where state-sponsored brutality was eagerly adopted, there were only rare incidents of energetic anti-Semitism in Italy. Even among members of the Fascist party, who in 1938 were formally instructed to interest themselves in 'the Jewish question', a mere eight hundred and sixty-four out of a membership of four hundred thousand answered the call to dutiful malice. Jews were, however, abruptly excluded both from the armed forces (though expert engineers sometimes had to be recalled, furtively, to solve difficult problems) and from national educational establishments. One not wholly unhappy consequence was that many of the best teachers were forced to teach small classes in private Jewish schools.

In 1940, Primo received the top mark in the quantitative analysis examination at the Chemical Institute. This result was not unexpected, nor unmerited, but it was achieved thanks, in part, to his having gained secret access to the room where the practical quizzes were being prepared. A quick sight of the apparatus was all an astute young man needed to be able to guess the nature of the imminent tests. He tipped off two of his closest friends, who later received the same high mark.

It was one thing for Primo to pass examinations, another to find a reputable supervisor for his thesis. Most of the qualified academic scientists were either active Fascists or wary trimmers. Fearful of rejection, he steeled himself to approach a Gentile professor, Nicola Dallaporta, in the street one night. As he tried, stammeringly, to make his case to be allowed to pursue his research, in spite of the laws, Professor Dallaporta said simply, in the words of Jesus, 'Follow me.'

In private, Dallaporta was briskly encouraging: 'Listen,' he said, 'do your thesis. Who gives a damn about the laws?' The same teacher was to come and see Primo soon after his return from Auschwitz. He told him that he had been chosen to survive in order to write *If This is a Man*. Never doubting Dallaporta's good intentions, Primo took his remark to be 'like a blasphemy': it would entail that God had granted privileges, by saving some and condemning others. 'I am obliged to say', he later told Ferdinando Camon, a Catholic friend, 'that the experience of Auschwitz hit me so hard that it drove out any remnant of religious education that I might have received.'

Although Dan Vittorio Segre observed after meeting him in 1982 that Levi was 'a stranger to Jewish culture' and that he had 'landed on a Jewish planet in Auschwitz with no preparation and no Jewish upbringing', Primo had certainly learnt something of Judaism when studying for his bar mitzvah, the ritual admission into manhood, during his early teens. As Segre recounts in his memorable autobiography, he himself had escaped the Nazis and served in the British army before emigrating to Israel. But Zionism no more inspired Primo than did orthodoxy. At the same time, if he was confirmed in his lack of religious faith, he was by no means divorced from his origins. He appears to have become 'more Jewish' as time went by. In his later, anguished years, he was known to frequent the synagogue in Turin, albeit self-effacingly. His loyalty to what he could not believe was strengthened by what he had endured. Belief in God, if he ever had it, had been quenched for ever. Such credulity is not essential to Jewish identity, which is more to do with conduct, and community, than with creed.

That Primo Levi was not sent to Auschwitz until 1944 was, as he says with truthful irony, a piece of 'good fortune'. The massive deportations and murders of most of European Jewry were already well advanced, but the German war-machine had become so over-stretched that physically strong or professionally useful Jews, in particular scientists, were not immediately murdered: it was their privilege to be worked to death, rather than to be slaughtered.

Italian Jews, who were not numerous, had remained largely inaccessible to the Nazis' exterminatory efficiency until the collapse of Mussolini's tyranny in 1943. Even after the Germans occupied the country, and began to treat their erstwhile allies with vindictive brutality, Jews were often sheltered by compatriots whose dislike of the Germans greatly exceeded any distaste for Jews. On the other hand, in the so-called 'Republic of Saló', a Fascist enclave in the north of the country, where Mussolini continued to rule a petty fiefdom under the aegis of the Germans, the hard core of his followers – conscious that their last days were at hand – conducted themselves with redoubled arrogance.

Hannah Arendt, in her *Eichmann in Jerusalem*, famously and recklessly suggested that European Jews went docilely into the gas chambers. She represents them as submissive and without the will or leadership to resist. This charge has proved as adhesive as it is tendentious. There were many instances of resistance against odds infinitely less favourable than those under which the fully armed forces of many countries of Europe, great and small, surrendered to Hitler. In any event, as Elie Wiesel has remarked, the supposed sheeplike behaviour of the Jews was nothing compared to the sheeplike obedience of their murderers.

Primo's family continued to live in anxious safety in Turin throughout the war. He himself might never have been deported had he not been captured, late in 1943, after a company of Fascist militiamen stumbled by chance on the mountain hideout where he and some of his friends had formed a group of partisans. Although of pacific manner and scholarly appearance, he had decided to take up arms and was sleeping with a pistol under his pillow. He managed to hide it in the ashes of the stove before he was arrested, or he might well have been shot on the spot.

As it was, he had a choice when he was interrogated. If he confessed to being a partisan, he faced summary execution; if he posed as a Jew in hiding, he would be less offensive to his captors. In fact he was promised by them that if he would admit to being Jewish, 'We'll send you to a concentration camp and you'll stay there for the rest of the war. In Italy we don't hand anybody over to the Germans.' In the light of this assurance, Primo elected to camouflage himself as the Jew that he really was.

No disparagement is intended in remarking that the strength of Primo Levi, in the camps and afterwards, was of a piece with a certain duplicity which enabled him to be both himself and what others did not suspect: an observer as alert, and aloof, as he was unblinking. The Italians have a disobliging saying, '*Piedmontese, fals' e cortese*' ('the Piedmontese, deceitful and courteous'); Primo did not, I think, lack a deceptive side. Scrupulous in the honesty of his account, and in his personal behaviour, he made a quiet point of being less naïve than he appeared: he was both what he seemed *and* something more. Instead of the self-pity which introspection can provoke, he made a habit of dispassionate self-regard: as he entered the nightmare of the camps, he noticed his own reactions and behaviour as if he were a specimen in an experiment.

He watched his fellow-inmates with equal attention and, in many cases, with a kind of courteous coldness. In 1986 he told Philip Roth: 'I had an intense wish to understand, I was constantly pervaded by a curiosity that somebody afterwards did, in fact, deem nothing less than cynical, the curiosity of the naturalist who finds himself transplanted into an environment that is monstrous, but new, monstrously new.' It was this novelty which led Primo later to say that his time in Auschwitz had been an 'adventure'. In some respects, *the* experience of his life had been his season in the inner circle of a man-made inferno.

There were those, like his friend Alberto and the noble Lorenzo, a civilian worker who for six months brought Primo the remains of his rations, for whom his love is unequivocal, but his attitude to others, notably the young Frenchman whom he calls 'Henri', comes close to censure. He says of him, with a palpable wince of distaste, that he admired the resourcefulness which procured his survival, but that he would not care to meet him again.

Henri's real name was Paul Steinberg. As he told Myriam Anissimov,

'I had to be very clever, and from the start I watched my subjects (those in power) coldly . . . Their intrinsic instability, in fact a genuine madness, was a constant danger . . . whose violent symptoms were utterly unpredictable even to those who knew them best . . . I practised all the circus arts – animal tamer, tightrope walker, and even conjuror. And at this game, I made rapid strides.'

There was, it seems, a blatancy about Steinberg's calculations which gave him, at least in Primo's eyes, something of the allure of a prostitute. When first arrested, he was not yet twenty years old (Primo was only a few years his senior). If Steinberg was shameless in his seductions of those in authority, he did not, so far as we are told, betray his fellow-inmates, still less behave towards them with the callousness of the Kapos. What is sometimes missed in Primo's account of the horrors he endured and observed is that they did not impel him to abandon, or much alter, the moral standards with which he arrived. He does say that 'If the Lagers had lasted longer, a new, harsh language would have been born,' a language in which it might be possible to denote exactly what it felt like to suffer beyond endurance. As it was, however, Primo had to use the old language, with its civilised nuances and moral undertones, with which to convey what we, the fortunate, can never know in our flesh.

When he speaks of a 'degenerate German engineer' giving warm water from the train engine to a father and mother so that they could bathe the little girl whom the same engineer knew that he was taking to her death, the fastidious disgust with which the adjective is weighted seems to saturate it with a new dimension of revulsion. Early in the narrative, we get a sense of the moral finesse of which, like his literary and scientific culture, the naked, shivering, tattooed Jew, Häftling 174517, cannot, and will not, be stripped.

Not the least of Primo's chilling accuracies is that with which he concedes that, for all his suffering, he never really reached 'the bottom'. The true witnesses, he remarks in his late book, *The Drowned and the Saved*, were 'those who breathed their last in the gas trucks and gas chambers, or died under machine-gun fire in Babi Yar, Riga, Minsk or Ponary . . .'

By virtue of his B.Sc. (Turin), and a capacity to speak German, Primo was able to pass crucial weeks in the warmth of the Laboratory; because he was lucky enough to get scarlet fever in time to be consigned to the camp hospital, he avoided the death march away from the camp on which so many of his fitter companions died. Whatever the monstrosity of what he witnessed, he knew, in the words of Goya, '*Eso no es lo peor*': this is not the worst of it. Perhaps, for Primo, that *was* the worst of it.

He repeatedly emphasised one very important, and often missed, point when he insisted that Auschwitz (and the other camps) 'had nothing to do with the war'. The constant use of the term 'war crime' has done more than anything else to obscure and falsify the nature of what was done to Primo Levi and to those even less fortunate than he. The mystification of a crime, like the allegation that it is unique, both dignifies and clouds what happened. Neither Primo nor anyone else has been able rationally to explain what drove the Germans specifically to crimes which may have been without parallel, but were scarcely without precedent. What would it be, after all, to give a reasonable account of the irrational? Primo realised that unfaltering description of the facts was as close as he, or anyone, was likely to come to an explanation of them. He regretted the obscurantism of, for particular instance, Paul Celan, but he would not, I think, have failed to nod grimly at the poet's famous line: '*Der Tod ist ein Meister aus Deutschland*' ('Death is sovereign in Germany').

The history of European anti-Semitism does not account for the Nazi cult of mass murder, but it is not irrelevant to it. What happened at Auschwitz was not *caused* by a centuries-old tradition of disparagement and humiliation, nor by the example of pious murders by the first Crusaders, especially the Germans, who rehearsed what they hoped to do to the Saracen armies in the Holy Land by massacring unarmed Jews in the Rhineland. However, as Ferdinando Camon mentioned, to Primo's surprise, 'There is something in Christian culture that recommends relations with "the other" with the sole purpose of achieving his conversion ... The fate of "the other" is considered as nothing compared to his conversion. If you look into this assertion, at the end of a certain time you can see extermination.'

Martin Luther's change of attitude, from geniality to scatological abuse, after the German Jews failed to rally to his new version of Christianity, does something to confirm Camon's notion. Luther's splenetic expression of his frustration supplied a fundamental warrant for German anti-Semitism.

What Alphonse Dupront called 'the myth of the Crusade' did

not die with the last Crusader. When the Popes granted dispensation from normal Christian morality in order to confound the Heathen, they inaugurated a kind of ruthlessness which has licensed the betrayal of civilisation, in the name of civilisation. This finds its iniquitous echo in Himmler's speech to his extermination squads. In it, the *Reichsführer* SS cloaks the unspeakable in the lineaments of a sacred mission.

After the war, Primo lived a peacefully tormented life in Turin until 1987. His book had not at first found a wide public, and only reluctant publishers, but by the end of his life he had become the venerated voice of those who had been to hell and back. His books eventually enjoyed the kind of success, and he the kind of renown, which might have filled another author with complacency. In fact, Primo's dismay at human cruelty, and the fear that he could never make his message sufficiently credible, filled his old age with unappeasable demons. The past came back in palpable form when he was diagnosed with prostate cancer. It was probably due to the effect of the chemicals he had to manhandle, without any protective clothing, in the Lager.

His dignity and irony had armed him with a terrible, wilful calmness, but he was never at ease. Knowing all the time that there was much that he could never express in words, he kept his voice down the better to make it carry. He had admired the solidarity of the Greek Jews in Auschwitz who never allowed themselves, as most national groups did, to be fractured into selfishness. If the Greeks were pious, they were also ruthless in their struggle (mostly vain) to survive. They were never resigned; no more was Primo. It is clear, from many studies, that belief in some ideology, religious or political, helped inmates to rise above despair. Reason alone was Primo's crutch. He was sustained by the abstract, entirely human discipline of a scientific mind. He willed himself to be the sane man to whom rage and hatred were futile, if understandable, responses to savagery. He resisted accusing all Germans of some kind of ethnic taint, since that would have been to lapse into a racism hardly distinguishable from Nazism. Nevertheless, he declared *If This is a Man* to be 'aimed at the Germans like a loaded weapon'.

It is widely believed that, like his fellow-survivor Jean Améry before him, Primo committed suicide. He fell from the third-floor landing of his flat to the hallway below. David Mendel, a retired consultant cardiologist, shrewd admirer and personal friend of Primo, is not so sure. He told me that the medication which Levi was taking *might* have caused dizziness and could have unbalanced him into falling. What is certain is that Primo *was* a man, and a rare one, and that he left behind a testament which will live as long as civilisation and barbarism continue their battle to master humanity.

FREDERIC RAPHAEL

Author's Preface

It was my good fortune to be deported to Auschwitz only in 1944, that is, after the German government had decided, owing to the growing scarcity of labour, to lengthen the average life span of the prisoners destined for elimination; it conceded noticeable improvements in the camp routine and temporarily suspended killings at the whim of individuals.

As an account of atrocities, therefore, this book of mine adds nothing to what is already known to readers throughout the world on the disturbing question of the death camps. It has not been written in order to formulate new accusations; it should be able, rather, to furnish documentation for a quiet study of certain aspects of the human mind. Many people – many nations – can find themselves holding, more or less wittingly, that 'every stranger is an enemy'. For the most part this conviction lies deep down like some latent infection; it betrays itself only in random, discon-nected acts, and does not lie at the base of a system of reason. But when this does come about, when the unspoken dogma becomes the major premiss in a syllogism, then, at the end of the chain, there is the Lager. Here is the product of a conception of the world carried rigorously to its logical conclusion; so long as the concep-tion subsists, the conclusion remains to threaten us. The story of the death camps should be understood by everyone as a sinister alarm-signal.

I recognise, and ask indulgence for, the structural defects of the book. Its origins go back, not indeed in practice, but as an idea, an intention, to the days in the Lager. The need to tell our story to 'the rest', to make 'the rest' participate in it, had taken on for us, before our liberation and after, the character of an immediate and violent impulse, to the point of competing with our other elementary needs. The book has been written to satisfy this need: first and foremost, therefore, as an interior liberation. Hence its fragmentary character: the chapters have been written not in logical succession, but in order of urgency. The work of tightening up is more studied, and more recent.

It seems to me unnecessary to add that none of the facts are invented.

PRIMO LEVI

If This is a Man

You who live safe
In your warm houses,
You who find, returning in the evening,
Hot food and friendly faces:
    Consider if this is a man
    Who works in the mud
    Who does not know peace
    Who fights for a scrap of bread
    Who dies because of a yes or a no.
    Consider if this is a woman,
    Without hair and without name
    With no more strength to remember,
    Her eyes empty and her womb cold
    Like a frog in winter.
Meditate that this came about:
I commend these words to you.
Carve them in your hearts
At home, in the street,
Going to bed, rising;
Repeat them to your children,
    Or may your house fall apart,
    May illness impede you,
    May your children turn their faces from you.

1 The Journey

I was captured by the Fascist Militia on 13 December 1943. I was twenty-four, with little wisdom, no experience and a decided tendency – encouraged by the life of segregation forced on me for the previous four years by the racial laws – to live in an unrealistic world of my own, a world inhabited by civilised Cartesian phantoms, by sincere male and bloodless female friendships. I cultivated a moderate and abstract sense of rebellion.

It had been by no means easy to flee into the mountains and to help set up what, both in my opinion and in that of friends little more experienced than myself, should have become a partisan band affiliated with the Resistance movement 'Justice and Liberty'. Contacts, arms, money and the experience needed to acquire them were all missing. We lacked capable men, and instead we were swamped by a deluge of outcasts, in good or bad faith, who came from the plain in search of a non-existent military or political organisation, of arms, or merely of protection, a hiding-place, a fire, a pair of shoes.

At that time I had not yet been taught the doctrine I was later to learn so hurriedly in the Lager: that man is bound to pursue his own ends by all possible means, while he who errs but once pays dearly. So that I can only consider the following sequence of events justified. Three Fascist Militia companies, which had set out in the night to surprise a much more powerful and dangerous band than ours, broke into our refuge one spectral snowy dawn and took me down to the valley as a suspect person.

During the interrogations that followed, I preferred to admit my status of 'Italian citizen of Jewish race'. I felt that otherwise I would be unable to justify my presence in places too secluded even for an evacuee; while I believed (wrongly as was subsequently seen) that the admission of my political activity would have meant torture and certain death. As a Jew, I was sent to Fossoli, near Modena, where a vast detention camp, originally meant for English and American prisoners of war, collected all the numerous categories of people not approved of by the new-born Fascist Republic.

At the moment of my arrival, that is, at the end of January 1944, there were about one hundred and fifty Italian Jews in the camp, but within a few weeks their number rose to over six hundred. For the most part they consisted of entire families captured by the Fascists or Nazis through their imprudence or following secret accusations. A few had given themselves up spontaneously, reduced to desperation by the vagabond life, or because they lacked the means to survive, or to avoid separation from a captured relation, or even – absurdly – 'to be in conformity with the law'. There were also about a hundred Yugoslavian military internees and a few other foreigners who were politically suspect.

The arrival of a squad of German SS men should have made even the optimists doubtful; but we still managed to interpret the novelty in various ways without drawing the most obvious conclusions. Thus, despite everything, the announcement of the deportation caught us all unawares.

On 20 February, the Germans had inspected the camp with care and had publicly and loudly upbraided the Italian commissar for the defective organisation of the kitchen service and for the scarce amount of wood distribution for heating; they even said that an infirmary would soon be opened. But on the morning of the 21st we learned that on the following day the Jews would be leaving. All the Jews, without exception. Even the children, even the old, even the ill. Our destination? Nobody knew. We should be prepared for

a fortnight of travel. For every person missing at the roll-call, ten would be shot.

Only a minority of ingenuous and deluded souls continued to hope; we others had often spoken with the Polish and Croat refugees and we knew what departure meant.

For people condemned to death, tradition prescribes an austere ceremony, calculated to emphasise that all passions and anger have died down, and that the act of justice represents only a sad duty towards society which moves even the executioner to pity for the victim. Thus the condemned man is shielded from all external cares, he is granted solitude and, should he want it, spiritual comfort; in short, care is taken that he should feel around him neither hatred nor arbitrariness, only necessity and justice, and by means of punishment, pardon.

But to us this was not granted, for we were many and time was short. And in any case, what had we to repent, for what crime did we need pardon? The Italian commissar accordingly decreed that all services should continue to function until the final notice: the kitchens remained open, the corvées for cleaning worked as usual, and even the teachers of the little school gave lessons until the evening, as on other days. But that evening the children were given no homework.

And night came, and it was such a night that one knew that human eyes would not witness it and survive. Everyone felt this: not one of the guards, neither Italian nor German, had the courage to come and see what men do when they know they have to die.

All took leave from life in the manner which most suited them. Some praying, some deliberately drunk, others lustfully intoxicated for the last time. But the mothers stayed up to prepare the food for the journey with tender care, and washed their children and packed the luggage; and at dawn the barbed wire was full of children's washing hung out in the wind to dry. Nor did they forget the diapers, the toys, the cushions and the hundred other small things which mothers remember and which children always need. Would you not do the same? If you and your child were going to be killed tomorrow, would you not give him to eat today?

In hut 6A old Gattegno lived with his wife and numerous children and grandchildren and his sons- and daughters-in-law. All the men were carpenters; they had come from Tripoli after many long journeys, and had always carried with them the tools of their trade, their kitchen utensils and their accordions and violins to play and dance to after the day's work. They were happy and pious folk. Their women were the first silently and rapidly to finish the preparations for the journey in order to have time for mourning. When all was ready, the food cooked, the bundles tied together, they unloosened their hair, took off their shoes, placed the Yahrzeit candles on the ground and lit them according to the customs of their fathers, and sat on the bare soil in a circle for the lamentations, praying and weeping all the night. We collected in a group in front of their door, and we experienced within ourselves a grief that was new for us, the ancient grief of the people that has no land, the grief without hope of the exodus which is renewed every century.

Dawn came on us like a betrayer; it seemed as though the new sun rose as an ally of our enemies to assist in our destruction. The different emotions that overcame us, of resignation, of futile rebellion, of religious abandon, of fear, of despair, now joined together after a sleepless night in a collective, uncontrolled panic. The time for meditation, the time for decision was over, and all reason dissolved into a tumult, across which flashed the happy memories of our homes, still so near in time and space, as painful as the thrusts of a sword.

31 The Journey

Many things were then said and done among us; but of these it is better that there remain no memory.

With the absurd precision to which we later had to accustom ourselves, the Germans held the roll-call. At the end the officer asked '*Wieviel Stück?*' The corporal saluted smartly and replied that there were six hundred and fifty 'pieces' and that all was in order. They then loaded us on to the buses and took us to Carpi station. Here the train was waiting for us, with our escort for the journey. Here we received the first blows: and it was so new and senseless that we felt no pain, neither in body nor in spirit. Only a profound amazement: how can one hit a man without anger?

There were twelve goods wagons for six hundred and fifty men; in mine we were only forty-five, but it was a small wagon. Here then, before our very eyes, under our very feet, was one of those notorious transport trains, those which never return, and of which, shuddering and always a little incredulous, we had so often heard speak. Exactly like this, detail for detail: goods wagons closed from the outside, with men, women and children pressed together without pity, like cheap merchandise, for a journey towards nothingness, a journey down there, towards the bottom. This time it is we who are inside.

Sooner or later in life everyone discovers that perfect happiness is unrealisable, but there are few who pause to consider the antithesis: that perfect unhappiness is equally unattainable. The obstacles preventing the realisation of both these extreme states are of the same nature: they derive from our human condition, which is opposed to everything infinite. Our ever-insufficient knowledge of the future opposes it: and this is called, in the one instance, hope, and in the other, uncertainty of the following day. The certainty of death opposes it: for it places a limit on every joy, but also on every grief. The inevitable material cares oppose it: for as they poison every lasting happiness, they equally assiduously distract us from our misfortunes and make our consciousness of them intermittent and hence supportable.

It was the very discomfort, the blows, the cold, the thirst, that kept us aloft in the void of bottomless despair, both during the journey and after. It was not the will to live, nor a conscious resignation; for few are the men capable of such resolution, and we were but a common sample of humanity.

The doors had been closed at once, but the train did not move until evening. We had learnt of our destination with relief. Auschwitz: a name without significance for us at that time, but it at least implied some place on this earth.

The train travelled slowly, with long, unnerving halts. Through the slit we saw the tall pale cliffs of the Adige Valley and the names of the last Italian cities disappear behind us. We passed the Brenner at midday of the second day and everyone stood up, but no one said a word. The thought of the return journey stuck in my heart, and I cruelly pictured to myself the inhuman joy of that other journey, with doors open, no one wanting to flee, and the first Italian names . . . and I looked around and wondered how many, among that poor human dust, would be struck by fate. Among the forty-five people in my wagon only four saw their homes again; and it was by far the most fortunate wagon.

We suffered from thirst and cold; at every stop we clamoured for water, or even a handful of snow, but we were rarely heard; the soldiers of the escort drove off anybody who tried to approach the convoy. Two young mothers, nursing their children, groaned night and day, begging for water. Our state of nervous tension made the hunger, exhaustion and lack of sleep seem less of a torment. But the hours of darkness were nightmares without end.

There are few men who know how to go to their deaths with dignity, and often they are not those whom one would expect. Few know how to remain silent and respect the silence of others. Our restless sleep was often interrupted by noisy and futile disputes, by curses, by kicks and blows blindly delivered to ward off some encroaching and inevitable contact. Then someone would light a candle, and its mournful flicker would reveal an obscure agitation, a human mass, extended across the floor, confused and continuous, sluggish and aching, rising here and there in sudden convulsions and immediately collapsing again in exhaustion.

Through the slit, known and unknown names of Austrian cities, Salzburg, Vienna, then Czech, finally Polish names. On the evening of the fourth day the cold became intense: the train ran through interminable black pine forests, climbing perceptibly. The snow was high. It must have been a branch line as the stations were small and almost deserted. During the halts, no one tried any more to communicate with the outside world: we felt ourselves by now 'on the other side'. There was a long halt in open country. The train started up with extreme slowness, and the convoy stopped for the last time, in the dead of night, in the middle of a dark silent plain.

On both sides of the track rows of red and white lights appeared as far as the eye could see; but there was none of that confusion of sounds which betrays inhabited places even from a distance. By the wretched light of the last candle, with the rhythm of the wheels, with every human sound, now silenced, we awaited what was to happen.

Next to me, crushed against me for the whole journey, there had been a woman. We had known each other for many years, and the misfortune had struck us together, but we knew little of each other. Now, in the hour of decision, we said to each other things that are never said among the living. We said farewell and it was short; everybody said farewell to life through his neighbour. We had no more fear.

The climax came suddenly. The door opened with a crash, and the dark echoed with outlandish orders in that curt, barbaric barking of Germans in command which seems to give vent to a millennial anger. A vast platform appeared before us, lit up by reflectors. A little beyond it, a row of lorries. Then everything was silent again. Someone translated: we had to climb down with our luggage and deposit it alongside the train. In a moment the platform was swarming with shadows. But we were afraid to break that silence: everyone busied himself with his luggage, searched for someone else, called to somebody, but timidly, in a whisper.

A dozen SS men stood around, legs akimbo, with an indifferent air. At a certain moment they moved among us, and in a subdued tone of voice, with faces of stone, began to interrogate us rapidly, one by one, in bad Italian. They did not interrogate everybody, only a few: 'How old? Healthy or ill?' And on the basis of the reply they pointed in two different directions.

Everything was as silent as an aquarium, or as in certain dream sequences. We had expected something more apocalyptic: they seemed simple police agents. It was disconcerting and disarming. Someone dared to ask for his luggage: they replied, 'luggage afterwards'. Someone else did not want to leave his wife: they said, 'together again afterwards'. Many mothers did not want to be separated from their children: they said 'good, good, stay with child'. They behaved with the calm assurance of people doing their normal duty of every day. But Renzo stayed an instant too long to say goodbye to Francesca, his fiancée, and with a single blow they knocked him to the ground. It was their everyday duty.

35 The Journey

In less than ten minutes all the fit men had been collected together in a group. What happened to the others, to the women, to the children, to the old men, we could establish neither then nor later: the night swallowed them up, purely and simply. Today, however, we know that in that rapid and summary choice each one of us had been judged capable or not of working usefully for the Reich; we know that of our convoy no more than ninety-six men and twenty-nine women entered the respective camps of Monowitz-Buna and Birkenau, and that of all the others, more than five hundred in number, not one was living two days later. We also know that not even this tenuous principle of discrimination between fit and unfit was always followed, and that later the simpler method was often adopted of merely opening both the doors of the wagon without warning or instructions to the new arrivals. Those who by chance climbed down on one side of the convoy entered the camp; the others went to the gas chamber.

This is the reason why three-year-old Emilia died: the historical necessity of killing the children of Jews was self-demonstrative to the Germans. Emilia, daughter of Aldo Levi of Milan, was a curious, ambitious, cheerful, intelligent child; her parents had succeeded in washing her during the journey in the packed car in a tub with tepid water which the degenerate German engineer had allowed them to draw from the engine that was dragging us all to death.

Thus, in an instant, our women, our parents, our children disappeared. We saw them for a short while as an obscure mass at the other end of the platform; then we saw nothing more.

Instead, two groups of strange individuals emerged into the light of the lamps. They walked in squads, in rows of three, with an odd, embarrassed step, head dangling in front, arms rigid. On their heads they wore comic berets and were all dressed in long striped overcoats, which even by night and from a distance looked filthy and in rags. They walked in a large circle around us, never drawing near, and in silence began to busy themselves with our luggage and to climb in and out of the empty wagons.

We looked at each other without a word. It was all incomprehensible and mad, but one thing we had understood. This was the metamorphosis that awaited us. Tomorrow we would be like them.

Without knowing how, I found myself loaded on to a lorry with thirty others; the lorry sped into the night at full speed. It was covered and we could not see outside, but by the shaking we could tell that the road had many curves and bumps. Are we unguarded? Throw ourselves down? It is too late, too late, we are all 'down'. In any case we are soon aware that we are not without guard. He is a strange guard, a German soldier bristling with arms. We do not see him because of the thick darkness, but we feel the hard contact every time that a lurch of the lorry throws us all in a heap. At a certain point he switches on a pocket torch and instead of shouting threats of damnation at us, he asks us courteously, one by one, in German and in pidgin language, if we have any money or watches to give him, seeing that they will not be useful to us any more. This is no order, no regulation: it is obvious that it is a small private initiative of our Charon. The matter stirs us to anger and laughter and brings relief.

2 On the Bottom

The journey did not last more than twenty minutes. Then the lorry stopped, and we saw a large door, and above it a sign, brightly illuminated (its memory still strikes me in my dreams): '*Arbeit Macht Frei*', work gives freedom.

We climb down, they make us enter an enormous empty room that is poorly heated. We have a terrible thirst. The weak gurgle of the water in the radiators makes us ferocious; we have had nothing to drink for four days. But there is also a tap – and above it a card which says that it is forbidden to drink as the water is dirty. Nonsense. It seems obvious that the card is a joke, 'they' know that we are dying of thirst and they put us in a room, and there is a tap, and '*Wassertrinken Verboten*'. I drink and I incite my companions to do likewise, but I have to spit it out, the water is tepid and sweetish, with the smell of a swamp.

This is hell. Today, in our times, hell must be like this. A huge, empty room: we are tired, standing on our feet, with a tap which drips while we cannot drink the water, and we wait for something which will certainly be terrible, and nothing happens and nothing continues to happen. What can one think about? One cannot think any more, it is like being already dead. Someone sits down on the ground. The time passes drop by drop.

We are not dead. The door is opened and an SS man enters, smoking. He looks at us slowly and asks, '*Wer kann Deutsch?*' One of us whom I have never seen, named Flesch, moves forward; he will be our interpreter. The SS man makes a long calm speech; the interpreter translates. We have to form rows of five, with intervals of two yards between man and man; then we have to undress and make a bundle of the clothes in a special manner, the woollen garments on one side, all the rest on the other; we must take off our shoes but pay great attention that they are not stolen.

Stolen by whom? Why should our shoes be stolen? And what about our documents, the few things we have in our pockets, our watches? We all look at the interpreter, and the interpreter asks the German, and the German smokes and looks him through and through as if he were transparent, as if no one had spoken.

I had never seen old men naked. Mr Bergmann wore a truss and asked the interpreter if he should take it off, and the interpreter hesitated. But the German understood and spoke seriously to the interpreter, pointing to someone. We saw the interpreter swallow and then he said: 'The officer says, take off the truss, and you will be given that of Mr Coen.' One could see the words coming bitterly out of Flesch's mouth; this was the German manner of laughing.

Now another German comes and tells us to put the shoes in a certain corner, and we put them there, because now it is all over and we feel outside this world and the only thing is to obey. Someone comes with a broom and sweeps away all the shoes, outside the door in a heap. He is crazy, he is mixing them all together, ninety-six pairs, they will be all unmatched. The outside door opens, a freezing wind enters and we are naked and cover ourselves up with our arms. The wind blows and slams the door; the German reopens it and stands watching with interest how we writhe to hide from the wind, one behind the other. Then he leaves and closes it.

Now the second act begins. Four men with razors, soap-brushes and clippers burst in; they have trousers and jackets with stripes, with a number sewn on the front; perhaps they are the same sort as those others of this evening (this evening or yesterday evening?); but these are robust and flourishing. We ask many questions but they catch hold of us and in a moment we find ourselves shaved and sheared. What comic faces we have without hair! The four speak a language which does not seem of this world. It is certainly not German, for I understand a little German.

Finally another door is opened: here we are, locked in, naked, sheared and standing, with our feet in water – it is a shower-room. We are alone. Slowly the astonishment dissolves, and we speak, and everyone asks questions and no one answers. If we are naked in a shower-room, it means that we will have a shower. If we have a shower it is because they are not going to kill us yet. But why then do they keep us standing, and give us nothing to drink, while nobody explains anything, and we have no shoes or clothes, but we are all naked with our feet in the water, and we have been travelling five days and cannot even sit down.

And our women?

Mr Levi asks me if I think that our women are like us at this moment, and where they are, and if we will be able to see them again. I say yes, because he is married and has a daughter; certainly we will see them again. But by now my belief is that all this is a game to mock and sneer at us. Clearly they will kill us, whoever thinks he is going to live is mad, it means that he has swallowed the bait, but I have not; I have understood that it will soon all be over, perhaps in this same room, when they get bored of seeing us naked, dancing from foot to foot and trying every now and again to sit down on the floor. But there are two inches of cold water and we cannot sit down.

We walk up and down without sense, and we talk, everybody talks to everybody else, we make a great noise. The door opens, and a German enters; it is the officer of before. He speaks briefly, the interpreter translates. 'The officer says you must be quiet, because this is not a rabbinical school.' One sees the words which are not his, the bad words, twist his mouth as they come out, as if he was spitting out a foul taste. We beg him to ask what we are waiting for, how long we will stay here, about our women, everything; but he says no, that he does not want to ask. This Flesch, who is most unwilling to translate into Italian the hard cold German phrases and refuses to turn into German our questions because he knows that it is useless, is a German Jew of about fifty, who has a large scar on his face from a wound received fighting the Italians on the Piave. He is a closed, taciturn man, for whom I feel an instinctive respect as I feel that he has begun to suffer before us.

The German goes and we remain silent, although we are a little ashamed of our silence. It is still night and we wonder if the day will ever come. The door opens again, and someone else dressed in stripes comes in. He is different from the others, older, with glasses, a more civilised face, and much less robust. He speaks to us in Italian.

By now we are tired of being amazed. We seem to be watching some mad play, one of those plays in which the witches, the Holy Spirit and the devil appear. He speaks Italian badly, with a strong foreign accent. He makes a long speech, is very polite, and tries to reply to all our questions.

We are at Monowitz, near Auschwitz, in Upper Silesia, a region inhabited by both Poles and Germans. This camp is a work-camp, in German one says *Arbeitslager*; all the prisoners (there are about ten thousand) work in a factory which produces a type of rubber called Buna, so that the camp itself is called Buna.

We will be given shoes and clothes – no, not our own – other shoes, other clothes, like his. We are naked now because we are waiting for the shower and the disinfection, which will take place immediately after the reveille, because one cannot enter the camp without being disinfected.

Certainly there will be work to do, everyone must work here.

But there is work and work: he, for example, acts as doctor. He is a Hungarian doctor who studied in Italy and he is the dentist of the Lager. He has been in the Lager for four and a half years (not in this one: Buna has only been open for a year and a half), but we can see that he is still quite well, not very thin. Why is he in the Lager? Is he Jewish like us? 'No,' he says simply, 'I am a criminal.'

We ask him many questions. He laughs, replies to some and not to others, and it is clear that he avoids certain subjects. He does not speak of the women: he says they are well, that we will see them again soon, but he does not say how or where. Instead he tells us other things, strange and crazy things, perhaps he too is playing with us. Perhaps he is mad – one goes mad in the Lager. He says that every Sunday there are concerts and football matches. He says that whoever boxes well can become cook. He says that whoever works well receives prize-coupons with which to buy tobacco and soap. He says that the water is really not drinkable, and that instead a coffee substitute is distributed every day, but generally nobody drinks it as the soup itself is sufficiently watery to quench thirst. We beg him to find us something to drink, but he says he cannot, that he has come to see us secretly, against SS orders, as we still have to be disinfected, and that he must leave at once; he has come because he has a liking for Italians, and because, he says, he 'has a little heart'. We ask him if there are other Italians in the camp and he says there are some, a few, he does not know how many; and he at once changes the subject. Meanwhile a bell rang and he immediately hurried off and left us stunned and disconcerted. Some feel refreshed but I do not. I still think that even this dentist, this incomprehensible person, wanted to amuse himself at our expense, and I do not want to believe a word of what he said.

At the sound of the bell, we can hear the still dark camp waking up. Unexpectedly the water gushes out boiling from the showers –

five minutes of bliss; but immediately after, four men (perhaps they are the barbers) burst in yelling and shoving and drive us out, wet and steaming, into the adjoining room which is freezing; here other shouting people throw at us unrecognisable rags and thrust into our hands a pair of broken-down boots with wooden soles; we have no time to understand and we already find ourselves in the open, in the blue and icy snow of dawn, barefoot and naked, with all our clothing in our hands, with a hundred yards to run to the next hut. There we are finally allowed to get dressed.

When we finish, everyone remains in his own corner and we do not dare lift our eyes to look at one another. There is nowhere to look in a mirror, but our appearance stands in front of us, reflected in a hundred livid faces, in a hundred miserable and sordid puppets. We are transformed into the phantoms glimpsed yesterday evening.

Then for the first time we became aware that our language lacks words to express this offence, the demolition of a man. In a moment, with almost prophetic intuition, the reality was revealed to us: we had reached the bottom. It is not possible to sink lower than this; no human condition is more miserable than this, nor could it conceivably be so. Nothing belongs to us any more; they have taken away our clothes, our shoes, even our hair; if we speak, they will not listen to us, and if they listen, they will not understand. They will even take away our name: and if we want to keep it, we will have to find ourselves the strength to do so, to manage somehow so that behind the name something of us, of us as we were, still remains.

We know that we will have difficulty in being understood, and this is as it should be. But consider what value, what meaning is enclosed even in the smallest of our daily habits, in the hundred possessions which even the poorest beggar owns: a handkerchief, an old letter, the photo of a cherished person. These things are part of us, almost like limbs of our body; nor is it conceivable that we can be deprived of them in our world, for we immediately find others to replace the old ones, other objects which are ours in their personification and evocation of our memories.

Imagine now a man who is deprived of everyone he loves, and at the same time of his house, his habits, his clothes, in short, of everything he possesses: he will be a hollow man, reduced to suffering and needs, forgetful of dignity and restraint, for he who loses all often easily loses himself. He will be a man whose life or death can be lightly decided with no sense of human affinity, in the most fortunate of cases, on the basis of a pure judgement of utility. It is in this way that one can understand the double sense of the term 'extermination camp', and it is now clear what we seek to express with the phrase: 'to lie on the bottom'.

*Häftling**: I have learnt that I am Häftling. My number is 174517; we have been baptised, we will carry the tattoo on our left arm until we die.

The operation was slightly painful and extraordinarily rapid: they placed us all in a row, and one by one, according to the alphabetical order of our names, we filed past a skilful official, armed with a sort of pointed tool with a very short needle. It seems that this is the real, true initiation: only by 'showing one's number' can one get bread and soup. Several days passed, and not a few cuffs and punches, before we became used to showing our number promptly enough not to disorder the daily operation of food distribution; weeks and months were needed to learn its sound in the German language. And for many days, while the habits of freedom still led me to look for the time on my wristwatch, my new name

* Prisoner.

ironically appeared instead, a number tattooed in bluish characters under the skin.

Only much later, and slowly, a few of us learnt something of the funereal science of the numbers of Auschwitz, which epitomise the stages of destruction of European Judaism. To the old hands of the camp, the numbers told everything: the period of entry into the camp, the convoy of which one formed a part, and consequently the nationality. Everyone will treat with respect the numbers from 30,000 to 80,000: there are only a few hundred left and they represented the few survivals from the Polish ghettos. It is as well to watch out in commercial dealings with a 116,000 or a 117,000: they now number only about forty, but they represent the Greeks of Salonica, so take care they do not pull the wool over your eyes. As for the High Numbers, they carry an essentially comic air about them, like the words 'freshman' or 'conscript' in ordinary life. The typical High Number is a corpulent, docile and stupid fellow: he can be convinced that leather shoes are distributed at the infirmary to all those with delicate feet, and can be persuaded to run there and leave his bowl of soup 'in your custody'; you can sell him a spoon for three rations of bread; you can send him to the most ferocious of the Kapos to ask him (as happened to me!) if it is true that his is the *Kartoffelschalenkommando*, the 'Potato Peeling Command', and if one can be enrolled in it.

In fact, the whole process of introduction to what was for us a new order took place in a grotesque and sarcastic manner. When the tattooing operation was finished, they shut us in a vacant hut. The bunks are made, but we are severely forbidden to touch or sit on them: so we wander around aimlessly for half the day in the limited space available, still tormented by the parching thirst of the journey. Then the door opens and a boy in a striped suit comes in, with a fairly civilised air, small, thin and blond. He speaks French and we throng around him with a flood of questions which till now we had asked each other in vain.

But he does not speak willingly; no one here speaks willingly. We are new, we have nothing and we know nothing; why waste time on us? He reluctantly explains to us that all the others are out at work and will come back in the evening. He has come out of the infirmary this morning and is exempt from work for today. I asked him (with an ingenuousness that only a few days later already seemed incredible to me) if at least they would give us back our toothbrushes. He did not laugh, but with his face animated by fierce contempt, he threw at me '*Vous n'êtes pas à la maison.*' And it is this refrain that we hear repeated by everyone. You are not at home, this is not a sanatorium, the only exit is by way of the Chimney. (What did it mean? Soon we were all to learn what it meant.)

And it was in fact so. Driven by thirst, I eyed a fine icicle outside the window, within hand's reach. I opened the window and broke off the icicle but at once a large, heavy guard prowling outside brutally snatched it away from me. '*Warum?*' I asked him in my poor German. '*Hier ist kein warum*' (there is no why here), he replied, pushing me inside with a shove.

The explanation is repugnant but simple: in this place everything is forbidden, not for hidden reasons, but because the camp has been created for that purpose. If one wants to live one must learn this quickly and well:

No Sacred Face will help thee here! it's not
A Serchio bathing-party . . .

Hour after hour, this first long day of limbo draws to its end. While the sun sets in a tumult of fierce, blood-red clouds, they finally make us come out of the hut. Will they give us something to drink? No, they place us in line again, they lead us to a huge square which takes up the centre of the camp and they arrange us meticulously in squads. Then nothing happens for another hour: it seems that we are waiting for someone.

A band begins to play, next to the entrance of the camp: it plays 'Rosamunda', the well-known sentimental song, and this seems so strange to us that we look, sniggering, at each other; we feel a shadow of relief, perhaps all these ceremonies are nothing but a colossal farce in Teutonic taste. But the band, on finishing 'Rosamunda', continues to play other marches, one after the other, and suddenly the squads of our comrades appear, returning from work. They walk in columns of five with a strange, unnatural hard gait, like stiff puppets made of jointless bones; but they walk scrupulously in time to the band.

They also arrange themselves like us in the huge square, according to a precise order; when the last squad has returned, they count and recount us for over an hour. Long checks are made which all seem to go to a man dressed in stripes, who accounts for them to a group of SS men in full battledress.

Finally (it is dark by now, but the camp is brightly lit by headlamps and reflectors) one hears the shout '*Absperre!*' at which all the squads break up in a confused and turbulent movement. They no longer walk stiffly and erectly as before: each one drags himself along with obvious effort. I see that all of them carry in their hand or attached to their belt a steel bowl as large as a basin.

We new arrivals also wander among the crowd, searching for a voice, a friendly face or a guide. Against the wooden wall of a hut two boys are seated on the ground: they seem very young, sixteen years old at the outside, both with their face and hands dirty with soot. One of the two, as we are passing by, calls me and asks me in

German some questions which I do not understand; then he asks where we come from. '*Italien*,' I reply; I want to ask him many things, but my German vocabulary is very limited.

'Are you a Jew?' I asked him.

'Yes, a Polish Jew.'

'How long have you been in the Lager?'

'Three years,' and he lifts up three fingers. He must have been a child when he entered, I think with horror; on the other hand this means that at least some manage to live here.

'What is your work?'

'*Schlosser*,' he replies. I do not understand. '*Eisen, Feuer*' (iron, fire), he insists, and makes a play with his hands of someone beating with a hammer on an anvil. So he is an ironsmith.

'*Ich Chemiker*,' I state; and he nods earnestly with his head, '*Chemiker gut.*' But all this has to do with the distant future: what torments me at the moment is my thirst.

'Drink, water. We no water,' I tell him.

He looks at me with a serious face, almost severe, and states clearly: 'Do not drink water, comrade,' and then other words that I do not understand.

'*Warum?*'

'*Geschwollen*,' he replies cryptically. I shake my head, I have not understood. '*Swollen*,' he makes me understand, blowing out his cheeks and sketching with his hands a monstrous tumefaction of the face and belly. '*Warten bis heute Abend.*' 'Wait until this evening,' I translate word by word.

Then he says: '*Ich Schlome. Du?*' I tell him my name, and he asks me: 'Where your mother?'

'In Italy.' Schlome is amazed: a Jew in Italy? 'Yes,' I explain as best I can, 'hidden, no one knows, run away, does not speak, no one sees her.' He has understood; he now gets up, approaches me and timidly embraces me. The adventure is over, and I feel filled with a serene sadness that is almost joy. I have never seen Schlome since, but I have not forgotten his serious and gentle face of a child, which welcomed me on the threshold of the house of the dead.

We have a great number of things to learn, but we have learnt many already. We already have a certain idea of the topography of the Lager; our Lager is a square of about 600 yards in length, surrounded by two fences of barbed wire, the inner one carrying a high-tension current. It consists of sixty wooden huts, which are called Blocks, ten of which are under construction. In addition, there is the body of the kitchens, which are in brick; an experimental farm, run by a detachment of privileged Häftlinge; the huts with the showers and the latrines, one for each group of six or eight Blocks. Besides these, certain Blocks are reserved for specific purposes. First of all, a group of eight, at the extreme eastern end of the camp, forms the infirmary and clinic; then there is Block 24 which is the *Krätzeblock*, reserved for infectious skin-diseases; Block 7 which no ordinary Häftling has ever entered, reserved for the '*Prominenz*', that is, the aristocracy, the internees holding the highest posts; Block 47, reserved for the *Reichsdeutsche* (the Aryan Germans, 'politicals' or criminals); Block 49, for the Kapos alone; Block 12, half of which, for use of the *Reichsdeutsche* and the Kapos, serves as a canteen, that is, a distribution centre for tobacco, insect powder and occasionally other articles; Block 37, which formed the Quartermaster's office and the Office for Work; and finally, Block 29, which always has its windows closed as it is the *Frauenblock*, the camp brothel, served by Polish Häftling girls, and reserved for the *Reichsdeutsche*.

The ordinary living Blocks are divided into two parts. In one *Tagesraum* lives the head of the hut with his friends. There is a long table, seats, benches, and on all sides a heap of strange objects in bright colours, photographs, cuttings from magazines, sketches, imitation flowers, ornaments; on the walls, great sayings, proverbs and rhymes in praise of order, discipline and hygiene; in one corner, a shelf with the tools of the *Blockfrisör* (official barber), the ladles to distribute the soup, and two rubber truncheons, one solid and one hollow, to enforce discipline should the proverbs prove insufficient. The other part is the dormitory: there are only one hundred and forty-eight bunks on three levels, fitted close to each other like the cells of a beehive, and divided by three corridors so as to utilise without wastage all the space in the room up to the roof. Here all the ordinary Häftlinge live, about two hundred to two hundred and fifty per hut. Consequently there are two men in most of the bunks, which are portable planks of wood, each covered by a thin straw sack and two blankets.

The corridors are so narrow that two people can barely pass together; the total area of the floor is so small that the inhabitants of the same Block cannot all stay there at the same time unless at least half are lying on their bunks. Hence the prohibition to enter a Block to which one does not belong.

In the middle of the Lager is the roll-call square, enormous, where we collect in the morning to form the work-squads and in the evening to be counted. Facing the roll-call square there is a bed of grass, carefully mown, where the gallows are erected when necessary.

We had soon learnt that the guests of the Lager are divided into three categories: the criminals, the politicals and the Jews. All are clothed in stripes, all are Häftlinge, but the criminals wear a green triangle next to the number sewn on the jacket; the politicals wear a red triangle; and the Jews, who form the large majority, wear the Jewish star, red and yellow. SS men exist but are few and outside the camp, and are seen relatively infrequently. Our effective masters in practice are the green triangles, who have a free hand over us, as well as those of the other two categories who are ready to help them – and they are not few.

And we have learnt other things, more or less quickly, according to our intelligence: to reply '*Jawohl*', never to ask questions, always to pretend to understand. We have learnt the value of food; now we also diligently scrape the bottom of the bowl after the ration and we hold it under our chins when we eat bread so as not to lose the crumbs. We, too, know that it is not the same thing to be given a ladleful of soup from the top or from the bottom of the vat, and we are already able to judge, according to the capacity of the various vats, what is the most suitable place to try and reach in the queue when we line up.

We have learnt that everything is useful: the wire to tie up our shoes, the rags to wrap around our feet, waste paper to (illegally) pad out our jacket against the cold. We have learnt, on the other hand, that everything can be stolen, in fact is automatically stolen as soon as attention is relaxed; and to avoid this, we had to learn the art of sleeping with our head on a bundle made up of our jacket and containing all our belongings, from the bowl to the shoes.

We already know in good part the rules of the camp, which are incredibly complicated. The prohibitions are innumerable: to approach nearer to the barbed wire than two yards; to sleep with one's jacket, or without one's pants, or with one's cap on one's head; to use certain washrooms or latrines which are '*nur für Kapos*' or '*nur für Reichsdeutsche*'; not to go for the shower on the prescribed day, or to go there on a day not prescribed; to leave the hut with one's jacket unbuttoned, or with the collar raised; to carry paper or straw under one's clothes against the cold; to wash except stripped to the waist.

The rites to be carried out were infinite and senseless: every morning one had to make the 'bed' perfectly flat and smooth; smear one's muddy and repellent wooden shoes with the appropriate machine grease; scrape the mudstains off one's clothes (paint, grease and rust-stains were, however, permitted); in the evening one had to undergo the control for lice and the control of washing one's feet; on Saturday, have one's beard and hair shaved, mend or have mended one's rags; on Sunday, undergo the general control for skin diseases and the control of buttons on one's jacket, which had to be five.

In addition, there are innumerable circumstances, normally irrelevant, which here become problems. When one's nails grow long, they have to be shortened, which can only be done with one's teeth (for the toe-nails, the friction of the shoes is sufficient); if a button comes off, one has to tie it on with a piece of wire; if one goes to the latrine or the washroom, everything has to be carried along, always and everywhere, and while one washes one's face, the bundle of clothes has to be held tightly between one's knees: in any other manner it will be stolen in that second. If a shoe hurts, one has to go in the evening to the ceremony of the changing of the shoes: this tests the skill of the individual who, in the middle of the incredible crowd, has to be able to choose at an eye's glance one (not a pair, one) shoe, which fits. Because once the choice is made, there can be no second change.

And do not think that shoes form a factor of secondary importance in the life of the Lager. Death begins with the shoes; for most of us, they show themselves to be instruments of torture, which after a few hours of marching cause painful sores which become fatally infected. Whoever has them is forced to walk as if he was dragging a convict's chain (this explains the strange gait of the army which returns every evening on parade); he arrives last everywhere, and everywhere he receives blows. He cannot escape if they run after him; his feet swell and the more they swell, the more the friction with the wood and the cloth of the shoes becomes insupportable. Then only the hospital is left: but to enter the hospital with a diagnosis of '*dicke Füsse*' (swollen feet) is extremely dangerous, because it is well known to all, and especially to the SS, that here there is no cure for that complaint.

And in all this we have not yet mentioned the work, which in its turn is a Gordian knot of laws, taboos and problems.

We all work, except those who are ill (to be recognised as ill implies in itself an important equipment of knowledge and experience). Every morning we leave the camp in squads for the Buna; every evening, in squads, we return. As regards the work, we are divided into about two hundred *Kommandos*, each of which consists of between fifteen and one hundred and fifty men and is commanded by a Kapo. There are good and bad Kommandos; for the most part they are used as transport and the work is quite hard, especially in the winter, if for no other reason merely because it always takes place in the open. There are also skilled Kommandos (electricians, smiths, bricklayers, welders, mechanics, concrete-layers, etc.), each attached to a certain workshop or department of the Buna, and depending more directly on civilian foremen, mostly German and Polish. This naturally only applies to the hours of work; for the rest of the day the skilled workers (there are no more than three or four hundred in all) receive no different treatment from the ordinary workers. The detailing of individuals to the various Kommandos is organised by a special office of the Lager, the *Arbeitsdienst*, which is in continual touch with the civilian direction of the Buna. The *Arbeitsdienst* decides on the basis of unknown criteria, often openly on the basis of protection or corruption, so that if anyone manages to find enough to eat, he is practically certain to get a good post at Buna.

53 On the Bottom

The hours of work vary with the season. All hours of light are working hours: so that from a minimum winter working day (8–12 a.m. and 12.30–4 p.m.) one rises to a maximum summer one (6.30–12 a.m. and 1–6 p.m.). Under no excuse are the Häftlinge allowed to be at work during the hours of darkness or when there is a thick fog, but they work regularly even if it rains or snows or (as occurs quite frequently) if the fierce wind of the Carpathians blows; the reason being that the darkness or fog might provide opportunities to escape.

One Sunday in every two is a regular working day; on the so-called holiday Sundays, instead of working at Buna, one works normally on the upkeep of the Lager, so that days of real rest are extremely rare.

Such will be our life. Every day, according to the established rhythm, *Ausrücken* and *Einrücken*, go out and come in; work, sleep and eat; fall ill, get better or die.

... And for how long? But the old ones laugh at this question: they recognise the new arrivals by this question. They laugh and they do not reply. For months and years, the problem of the remote future has grown pale to them and has lost all intensity in face of the far more urgent and concrete problems of the near future: how much one will eat today, if it will snow, if there will be coal to unload.

If we were logical, we would resign ourselves to the evidence that our fate is beyond knowledge, that every conjecture is arbitrary and demonstrably devoid of foundation. But men are rarely logical when their own fate is at stake; on every occasion, they prefer the extreme positions. According to our character, some of us are immediately convinced that all is lost, that one cannot live here, that the end is near and sure; others are convinced that however hard the present life may be, salvation is probable and not far off, and if we have faith and strength, we will see our houses and our dear ones again. The two classes of pessimists and optimists are not so clearly defined, however, not because there are many agnostics, but because the majority, without memory or coherence, drift between the two extremes, according to the moment and the mood of the person they happen to meet.

Here I am, then, on the bottom. One learns quickly enough to wipe out the past and the future when one is forced to. A fortnight after my arrival I already had the prescribed hunger, that chronic hunger unknown to free men, which makes one dream at night, and settles in all the limbs of one's body. I have already learnt not to let myself be robbed, and in fact if I find a spoon lying around, a piece of string, a button which I can acquire without danger of punishment, I pocket them and consider them mine by full right. On the back of my feet I already have those numb sores that will not heal. I push wagons, I work with a shovel, I turn rotten in the rain, I shiver in the wind; already my own body is no longer mine: my belly is swollen, my limbs emaciated, my face is thick in the morning, hollow in the evening; some of us have yellow skin, others grey. When we do not meet for a few days we hardly recognise each other.

We Italians had decided to meet every Sunday evening in a corner of the Lager, but we stopped it at once, because it was too sad to count our numbers and find fewer each time, and to see each other ever more deformed and more squalid. And it was so tiring to walk those few steps and then, meeting each other, to remember and to think. It was better not to think.

3 Initiation

After the first day of capricious transfer from hut to hut and from Kommando to Kommando, I am assigned to Block 30 late one evening, and shown a bunk in which Diena is already sleeping. Diena wakes up, and although exhausted, makes room for me and receives me hospitably.

I am not sleepy, or more accurately, my sleepiness is masked by a state of tension and anxiety of which I have not yet managed to rid myself, and so I talk and talk.

I have too many things to ask. I am hungry and when will they distribute the soup tomorrow? And will I be able to eat it without a spoon? And where will I be able to find one? And where will they send me to work? Diena knows no more than I, and replies with other questions. But from above and below, from near by and from far away, from all corners of the now-dark hut, sleepy and angry voices shout at me: '*Ruhe, Ruhe!*'

I understand that they are ordering me to be quiet, but the word is new to me, and since I do not know its meaning and implications, my inquietude increases. The confusion of languages is a fundamental component of the manner of living here: one is surrounded by a perpetual Babel, in which everyone shouts orders and threats in languages never heard before, and woe betide whoever fails to grasp the meaning. No one has time here, no one has patience, no one listens to you; we latest arrivals instinctively collect in the corners, against the walls, afraid of being beaten.

So I give up asking questions and soon slip into a bitter and tense sleep. But it is not rest: I feel myself threatened, besieged, at every moment I am ready to draw myself into a spasm of defence.

I dream and I seem to sleep on a road, on a bridge, across a door through which many people are passing. And now, oh, so early, the reveille sounds. The entire hut shakes to its foundations, the lights are put on, everyone near me bustles around in a sudden frantic activity. They shake the blankets, raising clouds of fetid dust, they dress with feverish hurry, they run outside into the freezing air half dressed, they rush headlong towards the latrines and washrooms. Some, bestially, urinate while they run to save time, because within five minutes begins the distribution of bread, of *bread-Brot-Broid-chleb-pain-lechem-keynér*, of the holy grey slab which seems gigantic in your neighbour's hand, and in your own hand so small as to make you cry. It is a daily hallucination to which in the end one becomes accustomed: but at the beginning it is so irresistible that many of us, after long discussions on our own open and constant misfortune and the shameless luck of others, finally exchange our ration, at which the illusion is renewed inverted, leaving everyone discontented and frustrated.

Bread is also our only money: in the few minutes which elapse between its distribution and consumption, the Block resounds with claims, quarrels and scuffles. It is the creditors of yesterday who are claiming payment in the brief moment in which the debtor is solvent. After which a relative quiet begins and many take advantage to go to the latrines again to smoke half a cigarette, or to the washrooms to wash themselves properly.

The washroom is far from attractive. It is badly lighted, full of draughts, with the brick floor covered by a layer of mud. The water is not drinkable; it has a revolting smell and often fails for many hours. The walls are covered by curious didactic frescos: for example, there is the good Häftling, portrayed stripped to the waist, about to diligently soap his sheared and rosy cranium, and the bad Häftling, with a strong Semitic nose and a greenish colour, bundled up in his ostentatiously stained clothes with a beret on his head, who cautiously dips a finger into the water of the washbasin. Under the first is written: '*So bist du rein*' (like this you are clean), and under the second: '*So gehst du ein*' (like this you come to a bad end); and lower down, in doubtful French but in Gothic script: '*La propreté, c'est la santé.*'

On the opposite wall an enormous white, red and black louse encamps, with the writing: '*Ein Laus, dein Tod*' (a louse is your death), and the inspired distich:

Nach dem Abort, vor dem Essen
Hände waschen, nicht vergessen.

(After the latrine, before eating, wash your hands, do not forget.)

For many weeks I considered these warnings about hygiene as pure examples of the Teutonic sense of humour, in the style of the dialogue about the truss which we had heard on our entry into the Lager. But later I understood that their unknown authors, perhaps without realising it, were not far from some very important truths. In this place it is practically pointless to wash every day in the turbid water of the filthy washbasins for purposes of cleanliness and health; but it is most important as a symptom of remaining vitality, and necessary as an instrument of moral survival.

I must confess it: after only one week of prison, the instinct for cleanliness disappeared in me. I wander aimlessly around the washroom when I suddenly see Steinlauf, my friend aged almost fifty, with nude torso, scrub his neck and shoulders with little success (he has no soap) but great energy. Steinlauf sees me and greets me, and without preamble asks me severely why I do not wash. Why should I wash? Would I be better off than I am? Would I please someone more? Would I live a day, an hour longer? I would probably live a shorter time, because to wash is an effort, a waste of energy and warmth. Does not Steinlauf know that after half an hour with the coal-sacks every difference between him and me will have disappeared? The more I think about it, the more washing one's face in our condition seems a stupid feat, even frivolous: a mechanical habit, or worse, a dismal repetition of an extinct rite. We will all die, we are all about to die: if they give me ten minutes between the reveille and work, I want to dedicate them to something else, to draw into myself, to weigh up things, or merely to look at the sky and think that I am looking at it perhaps for the last time; or even to let myself live, to indulge myself in the luxury of an idle moment.

But Steinlauf interrupts me. He has finished washing and is now drying himself with his cloth jacket which he was holding before wrapped up between his knees and which he will soon put on. And without interrupting the operation he administers me a complete lesson.

It grieves me now that I have forgotten his plain, outspoken words, the words of ex-sergeant Steinlauf of the Austro-Hungarian army, Iron Cross of the '14–'18 war. It grieves me because it means that I have to translate his uncertain Italian and his quiet manner of speaking of a good soldier into my language of an incredulous man. But this was the sense, not forgotten either then or later: that precisely because the Lager was a great machine to reduce us to beasts, we must not become beasts; that even in this place one can survive, and therefore one must want to survive, to tell the story, to bear witness; and that to survive we must force ourselves to save at least the skeleton, the scaffolding, the form of civilisation. We are slaves, deprived of every right, exposed to every insult, condemned to certain death, but we still possess one power, and we must defend it with all our strength for it is the last – the power to refuse our con-

sent. So we must certainly wash our faces without soap in dirty water and dry ourselves on our jackets. We must polish our shoes, not because the regulation states it, but for dignity and propriety. We must walk erect, without dragging our feet, not in homage to Prussian discipline but to remain alive, not to begin to die.

These things Steinlauf, a man of good will, told me; strange things to my unaccustomed ear, understood and accepted only in part, and softened by an easier, more flexible and blander doctrine, which for centuries has found its dwelling-place on the other side of the Alps; according to which, among other things, nothing is of greater vanity than to force oneself to swallow whole a moral system elaborated by others, under another sky. No, the wisdom and virtue of Steinlauf, certainly good for him, is not enough for me. In the face of this complicated world my ideas of damnation are confused; is it really necessary to elaborate a system and put it into practice? Or would it not be better to acknowledge one's lack of a system?

4 Ka-Be

The days all seem alike and it is not easy to count them. For days now we have formed teams of two, from the railway to the store – 100 yards over thawing ground. To the store, bending underneath the load, back again, arms hanging down one's sides, not speaking.

Around us, everything is hostile. Above us the malevolent clouds chase each other to separate us from the sun; on all sides the squalor of the toiling steel closes in on us. We have never seen its boundaries, but we feel all around us the evil presence of the barbed wire that separates us from the world. And on the scaffolding, on the trains being switched about, on the roads, in the pits, in the offices, men and more men, slaves and masters, the masters slaves themselves. Fear motivates the former, hatred the latter, all other forces are silent. All are enemies or rivals.

No, I honestly do not feel my companion of today, harnessed with me under the same load, to be either enemy or rival.

He is Null Achtzehn. He is not called anything except that, Zero Eighteen, the last three figures of his entry number; as if everyone was aware that only a man is worthy of a name, and that Null Achtzehn is no longer a man. I think that even he has forgotten his name, certainly he acts as if this was so. When he speaks, when he looks around, he gives the impression of being empty inside, nothing more than an involucre, like the slough of certain insects which one finds on the banks of swamps, held by a thread to the stones and shaken by the wind.

Null Achtzehn is very young, which is a grave danger. Not only because boys bear exhaustion and fasting worse than adults, but even more because a long training is needed to survive here in the struggle of each one against all, a training which young people rarely have. Null Achtzehn is not even particularly weak, but all avoid working with him. He is indifferent to the point of not even troubling to avoid tiredness and blows or to search for food. He carries out all the orders that he is given, and it is foreseeable that when they send him to his death he will go with the same total indifference.

He has not even the rudimentary astuteness of a draught-horse, which stops pulling a little before it reaches exhaustion: he pulls or carries or pushes as long as his strength allows him, then he gives way at once, without a word of warning, without lifting his sad, opaque eyes from the ground. He made me think of the sledge-dogs in London's books, who slave until the last breath and die on the track.

But as all the rest of us try by every possible means to avoid work, Null Achtzehn is the one who works more than all. It is because of this, and because he is a dangerous companion, that no one wants to work with him; and as, on the other hand, no one wants to work with me, because I am weak and clumsy, it often happens that we find ourselves paired together.

As we come back once again from the store, with hands empty, dragging our feet, an engine whistles briefly and cuts off our path. Happy at the enforced delay, Null Achtzehn and I stop; bent and in rags, we wait for the wagons to pass slowly by.

. . . *Deutsche Reichsbahn. Deutsche Reichsbahn. SNCF.* Two huge Russian goods wagons with the hammer and sickle badly rubbed off. Then, *Cavalli 8, Uomini 40, Tara, Portata*: an Italian wagon . . . Oh, to climb into a corner, well hidden under the coal, and to stay there quiet and still in the dark, to listen endlessly to the rhythm of the wheels, stronger than hunger or tiredness; until, at a certain moment, the train would stop and I would feel the warm air and the smell of hay and I would get out into the sun; then I would lie down on the ground to kiss the earth, as you read in books, with my face in the grass. And a woman would pass, and she would ask me 'Who are you?' in Italian, and I would tell her my story in Italian, and she would understand, and she would give me food and shelter. And she would not believe the things I tell her, and I would show her the number on my arm, and then she would believe . . .

. . . It is over. The last wagon has passed, and as if the curtain had been raised, the pile of cast-iron supports lies before our eyes. The Kapo on his feet at the pile with a switch in his hand, the wan companions who come and go in pairs.

Alas for the dreamer: the moment of consciousness that accompanies the awakening is the acutest of sufferings. But it does not often happen to us, and they are not long dreams. We are only tired beasts.

We are once again at the foot of the pile. Mischa and the Galician lift a support and put it roughly on our shoulders. Their job is the least tiring, so that they show excess zeal to keep it: they shout at companions who dawdle, they incite them, they admonish them, they drive on the work at an unbearable pace. This fills me with anger, although I already know that it is in the normal order of things that the privileged oppress the unprivileged: the social structure of the camp is based on this human law.

This time it is my turn to walk in front. The support is heavy but very short, so that at every step I feel behind me Null Achtzehn's feet which tread on mine, as he is unable or cannot be bothered to keep in step.

Twenty steps, we have arrived at the railroad, there is a cable to climb over. The load is badly placed, something is not right, it seems to be slipping from my shoulder. Fifty steps, sixty. The door of the store: still the same distance to walk and we can put it down. It is enough, I cannot go any further, the load is now weighing entirely on my arm. I cannot stand the pain and exhaustion any longer: I shout, I try to turn around, just in time to see Null Achtzehn trip and throw everything down.

If I had still had my agility of earlier days I could have jumped back: instead, here I am on the ground, with all my muscles contracted, the wounded foot tight between my hands, blind with pain. The corner of the piece of iron had cut across the back of my foot.

For a moment all is blank in the giddiness of pain. When I manage to look around, Null Achtzehn is still there on his feet, he has not moved, with his hands in his sleeves, his face expressionless, he does not say a word. Mischa and the Galician arrive, speaking Yiddish to each other, they give me incomprehensible advice. Templer and David and the others arrive: they profit from the distraction to stop work. The Kapo arrives, he distributes kicks, punches and abuse, and the comrades disperse like chaff in the wind. Null Achtzehn puts his hand to his nose and blankly looks at it, dirty with blood. I only receive two blows on the head, of the sort that do no harm but simply stun.

The incident is closed. It is proven, for good or bad, that I can stand up, so that the bone cannot be broken. I do not dare to cut the boot open for fear of wakening the pain again, and also because I know that the foot will swell and I will be unable to put the boot on again.

The Kapo sends me to take the place of the Galician at the pile, and the latter, glaring at me, takes his place alongside Null

Achtzehn; but by now the English prisoners have passed, it will soon be time to return to the camp.

During the march I do my best to walk quickly, but I cannot keep up the pace. The Kapo picks out Null Achtzehn and Finder to help me as far as the procession in front of the SS, and finally (fortunately there is no roll-call this evening) I am in the hut and I can throw myself on the bunk and breathe.

Perhaps it is the heat, perhaps the fatigue of the march, but the pain has begun again, together with a strange feeling of humidity in the wounded foot. I take off my shoe: it is full of blood, by now congealed and kneaded into the mud and rags of the cloth I found a month ago, and which I use as a foot-pad, one day on the right, one day on the left foot.

This evening, after soup, I will go to Ka-Be.

Ka-Be is the abbreviation of *Krankenbau*, the infirmary. There are eight huts, exactly like the others in the camp, but separated by a wire fence. They permanently hold a tenth of the population of the camp, but there are few who stay there longer than two weeks and none more than two months: within these limits they are held to die or be cured. Those who show signs of improvement are cured in Ka-Be, those who seem to get worse are sent from Ka-Be to the gas chambers. All this because we, fortunately, belong to the category of 'economically useful Jews'.

I have never been to Ka-Be nor to the clinic, and it is all new to me. There are two clinics, medical and surgical. In front of the door, exposed to the night and the wind, there are two long shadows. Some only have need of a bandage or a pill, others ask to be examined; some show death in their faces. Those at the front of both rows are already barefoot and ready to enter. Others, as their turn to enter approaches, contrive in the middle of the crush to loosen the haphazard laces and wire threads of their shoes and to unfold the precious foot-pads without tearing them; not too early, so as not to stand pointlessly in the mud in bare feet; not too late, so as not to lose their turn to enter, because it is rigorously forbidden to enter Ka-Be with shoes. A gigantic French Häftling, sitting in the porch between the doors of the two clinics, enforces respect for the prohibition. He is one of the few French officials of the camp. And do not think that to spend one's day among the muddy and broken shoes is a small privilege: it is enough to think of how many enter Ka-Be with shoes, and leave with no further need of them . . .

When my turn comes I manage miraculously to take off my shoes and rags without losing any of them, without letting my bowl and gloves be stolen, without losing my balance and keeping my beret in my hand all the time, as for no reason can one wear it on entering a hut.

I leave the shoes at the depot and am given the appropriate check, after which, barefoot and limping, my hands full of all my poor possessions that I dare not leave anywhere, I am admitted inside and join a new queue which ends in the examination rooms.

In this queue one progressively undresses so as to be naked when one arrives at the head, where a male nurse puts a thermometer under one's armpit. If anyone is dressed he loses his turn and goes back to join the queue. Everybody has to be given the thermometer, even if he only has a skin disease or toothache. In this way they make sure that whoever is not seriously ill will not submit himself to this complicated ritual for the sake of caprice.

My turn finally arrives and I am brought in front of the doctor. The nurse takes out the thermometer and presents me: '*Nummer 174517, kein Fieber.*' I do not need a long examination: I am immediately declared *Arztvormelder*. What it means I do not know, but this is certainly not the place to ask questions. I find myself thrown out, I get back my shoes and go back to the hut.

Chajim rejoices with me: I have a good wound, it does not seem dangerous, but it should be enough to guarantee me a discreet period of rest. I will spend the night in the hut with the others, but tomorrow morning, instead of going to work, I will have to show myself to the doctors for the definitive examination: this is what *Arztvormelder* means. Chajim is experienced in these matters and he thinks that I will probably be admitted tomorrow to Ka-Be. Chajim is my bed-companion and I trust him blindly. He is Polish, a religious Jew, learned in rabbinical law. He is about as old as I, a watchmaker by profession, and here in Buna works as a precision mechanic; so he is among the few who are able to preserve their dignity and self-assurance through the practice of a profession in which they are skilled.

And so it happened. After the reveille and the bread they called me out with three others from my hut. They took us to a corner of the roll-call square where there was a long queue, all the *Arztvormelder* of today; someone came and took away my bowl, spoon, beret and gloves. The others laughed. Did I not know that I had to hide them or leave them with someone, or best of all sell them, as they cannot be taken in Ka-Be? Then they look at my number and shake their heads: any stupidity is to be expected from one with so high a number.

Then they counted us, they made us undress outside in the cold, they took our shoes, they counted us again, and they made us take a shower. Then an SS man came, he looked at us without interest, stopping in front of one with a large hydrocele, whom he placed apart. After which they counted us again and made us take another shower, although we were still wet from the first one and some were trembling from a chill.

We are now ready for the definitive examination. Outside the window one can see the white sky and sometimes the sun; in this country one can look at it fixedly, through the clouds, as through a misty window. To judge by its position it must be past 2 p.m. Goodbye soup by now, and we have been on our feet for ten hours and naked for six.

This second medical examination is also extraordinarily rapid: the doctor (he has a striped suit like us, but with a white coat over it, with the number sewn on the coat, and he is much fatter than us) looks at and touches my swollen and bloody foot, at which I cry out from pain. Then he says: '*Aufgenommen, Block 23.*' I stand there with my mouth open, waiting for some other indication, but someone pulls me backwards brutally, throws a gown on my bare shoulders, gives me a pair of sandals and drives me out into the open.

A hundred yards away is Block 23; written on it is '*Schonungsblock*'. Who knows what it means? Inside they take off my gown and sandals and I find myself naked and last again in a queue of human skeletons – the inmates of today.

I have stopped trying to understand for a long time now. As far as I am concerned, I am by now so tired of standing on my wounded foot, still untended, so hungry and frozen, that nothing can interest me any more. This might easily be my last day and this room the gas chamber of which all speak, but what can I do about it? I might just as well lean against the wall, close my eyes and wait.

My neighbour cannot be Jewish. He is not circumcised and besides (this is one of the few things that I have so far learnt), so blond a skin, a face and a body so huge, are characteristics of non-Jewish Poles. He is a whole head taller than me but he has quite cordial features, as have only those who do not suffer from hunger.

I tried to ask him if he knew when they would let us enter. He turned to the nurse who resembled him like a twin and was smoking in the corner; they talked and laughed together without replying, as if I was not there. Then one of them took my arm and looked at my number and then both laughed still more strongly. Everyone knows that the 174,000s are the Italian Jews, the well-known Italian Jews who arrived two months ago, all lawyers, all with degrees, who were more than a hundred and are now only forty; the ones who do not know how to work, and let their bread be stolen, and are slapped from the morning to the evening. The Germans call them '*zwei linke Hände*' (two left hands), and even the Polish Jews despise them as they do not speak Yiddish.

The nurse points to my ribs to show the other, as if I was a corpse in an anatomy class: he alludes to my eyelids and my swollen cheeks and my thin neck, he stoops to press on my tibia with his thumb, and shows the other the deep impression that his finger leaves in the pale flesh, as if it was wax.

I wish I had never spoken to the Pole: I feel as if I had never in all my life undergone an affront worse than this. The nurse, meanwhile, seems to have finished his demonstration in his language which I do not understand and which sounds terrible. He turns to me, and in near-German, charitably, tells me the conclusion: '*Du Jude, kaputt. Du schnell Krematorium fertig.*' (You Jew, finished. You soon ready for crematorium.)

Some more hours pass before all the inmates are seen, are given a shirt and their details taken. I, as usual, am the last. Someone in a brand-new striped suit asks me where I was born, what profession I practised 'as a civilian', if I had children, what diseases I had had, a whole series of questions. What use could they be? Is this a complicated rehearsal to make fools of us? Could this be the hospital? They make us stand naked and ask us questions.

Finally the door is opened, even for me, and I can enter the dormitory.

Here as everywhere there are bunks on three levels, in three rows throughout the hut, separated by two narrow corridors. The bunks are one hundred and fifty, the patients two hundred and fifty; so there are two in almost all the bunks. The patients in the upper bunks, squashed against the ceiling, can hardly sit up; they lean out, curious to see the new arrivals of today. It is the most interesting moment of the day, for one always finds some acquaintances. I am assigned bunk number 10 – a miracle! It is empty! I stretch myself out with delight; it is the first time since I entered the camp that I have a bunk all to myself. Despite my hunger, within ten minutes I am asleep.

The life of Ka-Be is a life of limbo. The material discomforts are relatively few, apart from hunger and the inherent pains of illness. It is not cold, there is no work to do, and unless you commit some grave fault, you are not beaten.

The reveille is at 4 a.m., even for the patients. One has to make one's bed and wash, but there is not much hurry and little severity. The bread is distributed at half-past five, and one can cut it comfortably into thin slices and eat it lying down in complete peace; then one can fall asleep again until the soup is distributed at midday. Until about 4 p.m. it is *Mittagsruhe*, afternoon rest-time; then there is often the medical visit and dispensing of medicines, and one has to climb down from the bunks, take off one's shirt and file past the doctor. The evening ration is also served in bed, after which, at 9 p.m., all the lights are turned off except for the shaded lamp of the night guard, and there is silence.

. . . And for the first time since I entered the camp the reveille catches me in a deep sleep and its ringing is a return from nothingness. As the bread is distributed one can hear, far from the windows, in the dark air, the band beginning to play: the healthy comrades are leaving in squads for work.

One cannot hear the music well from Ka-Be. The beating of the big drums and the cymbals reach us continuously and monotonously, but on this weft the musical phrases weave a pattern only intermittently, according to the caprices of the wind. We all look at each other from our beds, because we all feel that this music is infernal.

The tunes are few, a dozen, the same ones every day, morning and evening: marches and popular songs dear to every German. They lie engraved on our minds and will be the last thing in Lager that we shall forget: they are the voice of the Lager, the perceptible expression of its geometrical madness, of the resolution of others to annihilate us first as men in order to kill us more slowly afterwards.

When this music plays we know that our comrades, out in the fog, are marching like automatons; their souls are dead and the music drives them, like the wind drives dead leaves, and takes the place of their wills. There is no longer any will: every beat of the drum becomes a step, a reflected contraction of exhausted muscles. The Germans have succeeded in this. They are ten thousand and they are a single grey machine; they are exactly determined; they do not think and they do not desire, they walk.

At the departure and the return march the SS are never lacking. Who could deny them their right to watch this choreography of their creation, the dance of dead men, squad after squad, leaving the fog to enter the fog? What more concrete proof of their victory?

Even those in Ka-Be recognise this departure and return from work, the hypnosis of the interminable rhythm, which kills thought and deadens pain; they have experienced it themselves and they will experience it again. But one had to escape from the enchantment, to hear the music from outside, as happened in Ka-Be, and as we think back now after the liberation and the rebirth, without obeying it, without enduring it, to understand what it was, for what meditated reason the Germans created this monstrous rite, and why even today, when we happen to remember some of those innocent songs, our blood freezes in our veins and we become aware that to escape from Auschwitz was no small fortune.

I have two neighbours in the adjoining bunk. They lie down all day and all night, side by side, skin against skin, crossed like the Pisces of the zodiac, so that each has the feet of the other beside his head.

One is Walter Bonn, a Dutchman, civilised and quite well mannered. He sees that I have nothing with which to cut my bread and loans me his knife, and then offers to sell it to me for half a ration of bread. I discuss the price and then turn it down, as I think that I will always find someone to lend me one here in Ka-Be, while outside it only costs a third of a ration. Walter is by no means less courteous because of this, and at midday, after eating his soup, he cleans his spoon with his mouth (which is a good rule before loaning it, so as to clean it and not to leave waste any traces of soup which may still be there) and spontaneously offers me it.

'What are you suffering from, Walter?'

'*Körperschwäche*', organic decay. The worst disease: it cannot be cured, and it is very dangerous to enter Ka-Be with such a diagnosis. If it had not been for the oedema of his ankles (and he shows me it) which hinders him from marching to work, he would have been very cautious about reporting ill.

I still have quite confused ideas about this kind of danger.

Everybody speaks about it indirectly, by allusions, and when I ask some question they look at me and fall silent.

Is it true what one hears of selections, of gas, of crematoria?

Crematoria. The other one, Walter's neighbour, wakes up startled and sits up: who is talking about the crematorium? what is happening? cannot a sleeping person be left in peace? He is a Polish Jew, albino, with an emaciated and good-natured face, no longer young. His name is Schmulek, he is a smith. Walter tells him briefly.

So, 'der Italeyner' does not believe in selections. Schmulek wants to speak German but speaks Yiddish; I understand him with difficulty, only because he wants to be understood. He silences Walter with a sign, he will see about persuading me:

'Show me your number: you are 174517. This numbering began eighteen months ago and applies to Auschwitz and the dependent camps. There are now ten thousand of us here at Buna-Monowitz; perhaps thirty thousand between Auschwitz and Birkenau. Wo sind die Andere? Where are the others?'

'Perhaps transferred to other camps?' I suggest.

Schmulek shakes his head, he turns to Walter.

'Er will nix verstayen,' he does not want to understand.

But destiny ordained that I was soon to understand, and at the expense of Schmulek himself. That evening the door of the hut opened, a voice shouted 'Achtung!' and every sound died out to give way to a leaden silence.

Two SS men enter (one of them has many chevrons, perhaps he is an officer?). One can hear their steps in the hut as if it was empty; they speak to the chief doctor, and he shows them a register, pointing here and there. The officer notes down in a book. Schmulek touches my knee:

'Pass' auf, pass' auf,' keep your eyes open.

The officer, followed by the doctor, walks around in silence, nonchalantly, between the bunks; he has a switch in his hand, and flicks at the edge of a blanket hanging down from a top bunk, the patient hurries to adjust it.

One has a yellow face; the officer pulls away his blankets, he starts back, the officer touches his belly, says, '*Gut, gut,*' and moves on.

Now he is looking at Schmulek; he brings out the book, checks the number of the bed and the number of the tattoo. I see it all clearly from above: he has drawn a cross beside Schmulek's number. Then he moves on.

I now look at Schmulek and behind him I see Walter's eyes, so I ask no questions.

The day after, in place of the usual group of patients who have recovered, two distinct groups are led out. The first have been shaved and sheared and have had a shower. The second left as they are, with long hair and without being treated, without a shower. Nobody said goodbye to the latter, nobody gave them messages for healthy comrades.

Schmulek formed part of this group.

In this discreet and composed manner, without display or anger, massacre moves through the huts of Ka-Be every day, touching here and there. When Schmulek left, he gave me his spoon and knife; Walter and I avoided looking at each other and remained silent for a long time. Then Walter asked me how I manage to keep my ration of bread so long, and explained to me that he usually cuts his bread lengthwise to have longer slices in order to smear on the margarine more easily.

Walter explains many things to me: *Schonungsblock* means the rest hut, where there are only the less serious patients or convalescents, or those not requiring attention. Among them, at least fifty more or less serious dysentery patients.

These are checked every third day. They are placed in a line along the corridor. At the end there are two tin-plate pots, and the nurse with a register, watch and pencil. Two at a time, the patients present themselves and have to show, on the spot and at once, that they still have diarrhoea; to prove it, they are given exactly one minute. After which, they show the result to the nurse who looks at it and judges. They wash the pots quickly in a washtub near by and the next two take over.

Of those waiting, some are contorted in the pain of keeping in their precious evidence another ten, another twenty minutes; others, without resources at the moment, strain veins and muscles in a contrary effort. The nurse watches, impassive, chewing his pencil, one eye on the watch, one eye on the specimens gradually presented him. In doubtful cases, he leaves with the pot to show it to the doctor.

I receive an unexpected visit: it is Piero Sonnino, my friend from Rome. 'Have you seen how I have fixed it?' Piero has mild enteritis, has been here for twenty days, and is quite happy, rested and growing fatter; he could not care less about the selections and has decided to stay in Ka-Be until the end of the winter, at all costs. His method consists of placing himself in line behind some authentic dysentery patient who offers a guarantee of success; when it is his turn he asks for his collaboration (to be rewarded with soup or bread), and if the latter agrees, and the nurse has a moment of inattention, he switches over the pots in the middle of the crowd, and the deed is done. Piero knows what he is risking, but it has gone well so far.

But life in Ka-Be is not this. It is not the crucial moments of the selections, it is not the grotesque episodes of the diarrhoea and lice controls, it is not even the illnesses.

75 Ka-Be

Ka-Be is the Lager without its physical discomforts. So that, whoever still has some seeds of conscience, feels his conscience reawaken; and in the long empty days, one speaks of other things than hunger and work and one begins to consider what they have made us become, how much they have taken away from us, what this life is. In this Ka-Be, an enclosure of relative peace, we have learnt that our personality is fragile, that it is much more in danger than our life; and the old wise ones, instead of warning us 'remember that you must die', would have done much better to remind us of this great danger that threatens us. If from inside the Lager, a message could have seeped out to free men, it would have been this: take care not to suffer in your own homes what is inflicted on us here.

When one works, one suffers and there is no time to think: our homes are less than a memory. But here the time is ours: from bunk to bunk, despite the prohibition, we exchange visits and we talk and we talk. The wooden hut, crammed with suffering humanity, is full of words, memories and of another pain. '*Heimweh*' the Germans call this pain; it is a beautiful word, it means 'longing for one's home'.

We know where we come from; the memories of the world outside crowd our sleeping and our waking hours, we become aware, with amazement, that we have forgotten nothing, every memory evoked rises in front of us painfully clear.

But where we are going we do not know. Will we perhaps be able to survive the illnesses and escape the selections, perhaps even resist the work and hunger which wear us out – but then, afterwards? Here, momentarily far away from the curses and the blows, we can re-enter into ourselves and meditate, and then it becomes clear that we will not return. We travelled here in the sealed wagons; we saw our women and our children leave towards nothingness; we, transformed into slaves, have marched a hundred times backwards and forwards to our silent labours, killed in our spirit long before our anonymous death. No one must leave here and so carry to the world, together with the sign impressed on his skin, the evil tidings of what man's presumption made of man in Auschwitz.

5 Our Nights

After twenty days of Ka-Be, when my wound was practically healed, I was discharged to my great displeasure.

The ceremony is simple, but implies a painful and dangerous period of readjustment. All who have no special contacts are not returned to their former Block and Kommando on leaving Ka-Be, but are enrolled, on the basis of criteria wholly unknown to me, in any other hut and given any kind of work. Moreover, they leave Ka-Be naked; they are given 'new' clothes and shoes (I mean not those left behind at their entry) which need to be adapted with speed and diligence to their own persons, which implies effort and expense. They have to worry about acquiring a new spoon and knife as at the beginning. And finally – and this is the gravest aspect – they find themselves inserted in an unknown environment, among hostile companions never seen before, with leaders whose characters they do not know and against whom it is consequently difficult to guard themselves.

Man's capacity to dig himself in, to secrete a shell, to build around himself a tenuous barrier of defence, even in apparently desperate circumstances, is astonishing and merits a serious study. It is based on an invaluable activity of adaptation, partly passive and unconscious, partly active: of hammering in a nail above his bunk from which to hang up his shoes; of concluding tacit pacts of non-aggression with neighbours; of understanding and accepting the customs and laws of a single Kommando, a single Block. By virtue of this work, one manages to gain a certain equilibrium after a few weeks, a certain degree of security in face of the unforeseen; one has made oneself a nest, the trauma of the transplantation is over.

But the man who leaves the Ka-Be, naked and almost always insufficiently cured, feels himself ejected into the dark and cold of sidereal space. His trousers fall down, his shoes hurt him, his shirt has no buttons. He searches for a human contact and only finds backs turned on him. He is as helpless and vulnerable as a new-born baby, but the following morning he will still have to march to work.

It is in these conditions that I find myself when the nurse entrusts me, after various administrative rites, to the care of the *Blockältester* of Block 45. But at once a thought fills me with joy: I am in luck, this is Alberto's Block.

Alberto is my best friend. He is only twenty-two, two years younger than me, but none of us Italians have shown an equal capacity for adaptation. Alberto entered the Lager with his head high, and lives in here unscathed and uncorrupted. He understood before any of us that this life is war; he permitted himself no indulgences, he lost no time complaining and commiserating with himself and with others, but entered the battle from the beginning. He has the advantage of intelligence and intuition: he reasons correctly, often he does not even reason but is equally right. He understands everything at once: he knows a little French but understands whatever the Germans and Poles tell him. He replies in Italian and with gestures, he makes himself understood and at once wins sympathy. He fights for his life but still remains everybody's friend. He 'knows' whom to corrupt, whom to avoid, whose compassion to arouse, whom to resist.

Yet (and it is for this virtue of his that his memory is still dear and close to me) he himself did not become corrupt. I always saw, and still see in him, the rare figure of the strong yet peace-loving man against whom the weapons of night are blunted.

But I did not manage to gain permission to sleep in a bunk with him, and not even Alberto succeeded, although by now he enjoyed a certain popularity in Block 45. It is a pity, because to have a bed-companion whom one can trust, or at least with whom one can reach an understanding, is an inestimable advantage; and besides, it is winter now and the nights are long, and since we are forced to exchange sweats, smells and warmth with someone under the same blanket, and in a width little more than two feet, it is quite desirable that he be a friend.

In the winter the nights are long and we are allowed a considerable interval of time to sleep.

The tumult of the Block dies down; the distribution of the evening ration ended over an hour ago, and only a few stubborn people continue to scrape the by-now shining bottom of the bowl, turning it around with care under the lamp, frowning with attention. Engineer Kardos moves around the bunks, tending wounded feet and suppurating corns. This is his trade: there is no one who will not willingly renounce a slice of bread to soothe the torment of those numbed sores which bleed at every step all day. And so, in this manner, honestly, engineer Kardos solves the problem of living.

From the outside door, secretly and looking around cautiously, the story-teller comes in. He is seated on Wachsmann's bunk and at once gathers around him a small, attentive, silent crowd. He chants an interminable Yiddish rhapsody, always the same one, in rhymed quatrains, of a resigned and penetrating melancholy (but perhaps I only remember it so because of the time and the place that I heard it?); from the few words that I understand, it must be a song that he composed himself, in which he has enclosed all the life of the Lager in minute detail. Some are generous and give the story-teller a pinch of tobacco or a needleful of thread; others listen intently but give nothing.

The bell rings suddenly for the last ceremony of the day: '*Wer hat kaputt die Schuhe?*' (who has broken shoes?), and at once the noise of forty or fifty claimants to the exchange breaks out as they rush towards the *Tagesraum* in desperate haste, well knowing that only the first ten, on the best of hypotheses, will be satisfied.

Then there is quiet. The light goes out a first time for a few seconds to warn the tailors to put away the precious needle and thread; then the bell sounds in the distance, the night guard installs himself and all the lights are turned out definitively. There is nothing to do but to undress and go to bed.

I do not know who my neighbour is; I am not even sure that it is always the same person because I have never seen his face except for a few seconds amidst the uproar of the reveille, so that I know his back and his feet much better than his face. He does not work in my Kommando and only comes into the bunk at curfew time; he wraps himself in the blanket, pushes me aside with a blow from his bony hips, turns his back on me and at once begins to snore. Back against back, I struggle to regain a reasonable area of the straw mattress: with the base of my back I exercise a progressive pressure against his back; then I turn around and try to push with my knees; I take hold of his ankles and try to place them a little further over so as not to have his feet next to my face. But it is all in vain: he is much heavier than me and seems turned to stone in his sleep.

So I adapt myself to lie like this, forced into immobility, half-lying on the wooden edge. Nevertheless I am so tired and stunned that I, too, soon fall asleep, and I seem to be sleeping on the tracks of a railroad.

The train is about to arrive: one can hear the engine panting, it is my neighbour. I am not yet so asleep as not to be aware of the double nature of the engine. It is, in fact, the very engine which towed the wagons we had to unload in Buna today. I recognise it by the fact that even now, as when it passed close by us, I feel the heat it radiates from its black side. It is puffing, it is ever nearer, it is on the point of running over me, but instead it never arrives. My sleep is very light, it is a veil, if I want I can tear it. I will do it, I want to tear it, so that I can get off the railway track. Now I have done it and now I am awake: but not really awake, only a little more, one step higher on the ladder between the unconscious and the conscious. I have my eyes closed and I do not want to open them lest my sleep escape me, but I can register noises: I am sure this distant whistle is real, it does not come from an engine in a dream, it can be heard objectively. It is the whistle of the small-gauge track, it comes from the yard where they work at night as well. A long, firm note, then another one a semitone lower, then again the first, but short and cut off. This whistle is an important thing and in some ways essential: we have heard it so often associated with the suffering of the work and the camp that it has become a symbol and immediately evokes its image like certain music or smells.

This is my sister here, with some unidentifiable friend and many other people. They are all listening to me and it is this very story that I am telling: the whistle of three notes, the hard bed, my neighbour whom I would like to move, but whom I am afraid to wake as he is stronger than me. I also speak diffusely of our hunger and of the lice control, and of the Kapo who hit me on the nose and then sent me to wash myself as I was bleeding. It is an intense pleasure, physical, inexpressible, to be at home, among friendly people and to have so many things to recount: but I cannot help noticing that my listeners do not follow me. In fact, they are completely indifferent: they speak confusedly of other things among themselves, as if I was not there. My sister looks at me, gets up and goes away without a word.

A desolating grief is now born in me, like certain barely remembered pains of one's early infancy. It is pain in its pure state, not tempered by a sense of reality and by the intrusion of extraneous circumstances, a pain like that which makes children cry; and it is better for me to swim once again up to the surface, but this time I deliberately open my eyes to have a guarantee in front of me of being effectively awake.

My dream stands in front of me, still warm, and although awake I am still full of its anguish: and then I remember that it is not a haphazard dream, but that I have dreamed it not once but many times since I arrived here, with hardly any variations of environment or details. I am now quite awake and I remember that I have recounted it to Alberto and that he confided to me, to my amazement, that it is also his dream and the dream of many others, perhaps of everyone. Why does it happen? Why is the pain of every day translated so constantly into our dreams, in the ever-repeated scene of the unlistened-to story?

While I meditate on this, I try to profit from the interval of wakefulness to shake off the painful remnants of the preceding sleep, so as not to compromise the quality of the next dream. I crouch in the dark, I look around and I listen.

One can hear the sleepers breathing and snoring; some groan and speak. Many lick their lips and move their jaws. They are dreaming of eating; this is also a collective dream. It is a pitiless dream which the creator of the Tantalus myth must have known. You not only see the food, you feel it in your hands, distinct and concrete, you are aware of its rich and striking smell; someone in the dream even holds it up to your lips, but every time a different circumstance intervenes to prevent the consummation of the act. Then the dream dissolves and breaks up into its elements, but it reforms itself immediately after and begins again, similar, yet changed; and this without pause, for all of us, every night and for the whole of our sleep.

It must be later than 11 p.m. because the movement to and from the bucket next to the night guard is already intense. It is an obscene torment and an indelible shame: every two or three hours we have to get up to discharge ourselves of the great dose of water which during the day we are forced to absorb in the form of soup in order to satisfy our hunger: that same water which in the evenings swells our ankles and the hollows of our eyes, conferring on all physiognomies a likeness of deformation, and whose elimination imposes an enervating toil on our kidneys.

It is not merely a question of a procession to a bucket; it is the rule that the last user of the bucket goes and empties it in the latrines; it is also the rule that at night one must not leave the hut except in night uniform (shirt and pants), giving one's number to the guard. It is easily foreseeable that the night guard will try to exempt his friends, his co-nationals and the Prominents from this duty. Add to this that the old members of the camp have refined their senses to such a degree that, while still in their bunks, they are miraculously able to distinguish if the level is at a dangerous point, purely on the basis of the sound that the sides of the bucket make – with the result that they almost always manage to avoid emptying it. So the candidates for the bucket service are a fairly limited number in each hut, while the total volume to eliminate is at least forty gallons, which means that the bucket has to be emptied about twenty times.

In short, the risk which hangs over us, the inexperienced and non-privileged, when we are driven by necessity to the bucket every night is quite serious. The night guard unexpectedly jumps from his corner and seizes us, scribbles down our number, hands us a pair of wooden shoes and the bucket and drives us out into the middle of the snow, shivering and sleepy. It is our task to shuffle to the latrine with the bucket which knocks against our bare calves, disgustingly warm; it is full beyond all reasonable limit, and inevitably with the shaking some of the content overflows on our feet, so that however repugnant this duty may be, it is always preferable that we, and not our neighbour, be ordered to do it.

So our nights drag on. The dream of Tantalus and the dream of the story are woven into a texture of more indistinct images: the suffering of the day, composed of hunger, blows, cold, exhaustion, fear and promiscuity, turns at night-time into shapeless nightmares of unheard-of violence, which in free life would only occur during a fever. One wakes up at every moment, frozen with terror, shaking in every limb, under the impression of an order shouted out by a voice full of anger in a language not understood. The procession to the bucket and the thud of bare heels on the wooden floor turns into another symbolic procession: it is us again, grey and identical, small as ants, yet so huge as to reach up to the stars, bound one against the other, countless, covering the plain as far as the horizon; sometimes melting into a single substance, a sorrowful turmoil in which we all feel ourselves trapped and suffocated; sometimes marching in a circle, without beginning or end, with a blinding giddiness and a sea of nausea rising from the praecordia to the gullet; until hunger or cold or the fullness of our bladders turn our dreams into their customary forms. We try in vain, when the nightmare itself or the discomforts wake us, to extricate the various elements and drive them back, separately, out of the field of our present attention, so as to defend our sleep from their intrusion: but as soon as we close our eyes, once again we feel our brain start up, beyond our control; it knocks and hums, incapable of rest, it fabricates phantasms and ter-

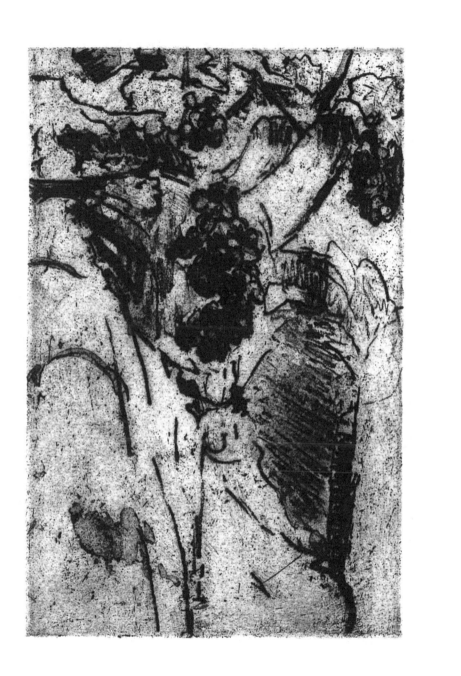

rible symbols, and without rest projects and shapes their images, as a grey fog, on to the screen of our dreams.

But for the whole duration of the night, cutting across the alternating sleep, waking and nightmares, the expectancy and terror of the moment of the reveille keeps watch. By means of that mysterious faculty of which many are aware, even without watches we are able to calculate the moment with close accuracy. At the hour of the reveille, which varies from season to season but always falls a fair time before dawn, the camp bell rings for a long time, and the night guard in every hut goes off duty; he switches on the light, gets up, stretches himself and pronounces the daily condemnation: '*Aufstehen,*' or more often in Polish: '*Wstavac*'.

Very few sleep on till the *Wstavac*: it is a moment of too acute pain for even the deepest sleep not to dissolve as it approaches. The night guard knows it and for this reason does not utter it in a tone of command, but with the quiet and subdued voice of one who knows that the announcement will find all ears waiting, and will be heard and obeyed.

Like a stone the foreign word falls to the bottom of every soul. 'Get up': the illusory barrier of the warm blankets, the thin armour of sleep, the nightly evasion with its very torments drops to pieces around us, and we find ourselves mercilessly awake, exposed to insult, atrociously naked and vulnerable. A day begins like every day, so long as not to allow us reasonably to conceive its end, so much cold, so much hunger, so much exhaustion separate us from it: so that it is better to concentrate one's attention and desires on the block of grey bread, which is small but which will certainly be ours in an hour, and which for five minutes, until we have devoured it, will form everything that the law of the place allows us to possess.

*

At the *Wstavac* the hurricane starts up again. The entire hut enters without transition into frantic activity: everybody climbs up and down, remakes his bed and tries at the same time to dress himself in a manner so as to leave none of his objects unguarded; the air is filled with so much dust as to become opaque; the quickest ones elbow their way through the crowd to go to the washroom and latrine before the queue begins. The hut-sweepers at once come on to the scene and drive everyone out, hitting and shouting at them.

When I have remade my bed and am dressed, I climb down on to the floor and put on my shoes. The sores on my feet reopen at once, and a new day begins.

6 The Work

Before Resnyk came, I slept with a Pole whose name no one knew; he was gentle and silent, with two old sores on his shin-bones, and during the night gave out a squalid smell of illness; he also had a weak bladder, and so woke up and woke me up eight or ten times a night.

One night he left his gloves in my care and entered the hospital. For half an hour I hoped that the Quartermaster would forget that I was the sole occupant of my bunk, but when the curfew bell had already sounded, the bed trembled and a long, red-haired fellow, with the number of the French of Drancy, climbed up beside me.

To have a bed-companion of tall stature is a misfortune and means losing hours of sleep; I always have tall companions as I am small and two tall ones cannot sleep together. But it could at once be seen that Resnyk, despite everything, was not a bad companion. He spoke little and courteously, he was clean, he did not snore, did not get up more than two or three times a night and always with great delicacy. In the morning he offered to make the bed (this is a complicated and difficult operation, and also carries a notable responsibility, as those who remake the bed badly, the 'schlechte Bettenbauer', are diligently punished) and did it quickly and well; so that I experienced a certain fleeting pleasure later in the roll-call square on seeing that he had been assigned to my Kommando.

On the march to work, limping in our large wooden shoes on the icy snow, we exchanged a few words, and I found out that Resnyk is Polish; he lived twenty years at Paris but speaks an incredible French. He is thirty, but like all of us, could be taken for seventeen or fifty. He told me his story, and today I have forgotten it, but it was certainly a sorrowful, cruel and moving story; because so are all our stories, hundreds of thousands of stories, all different and all full of a tragic, disturbing necessity. We tell them to each other in the evening, and they take place in Norway, Italy, Algeria, the Ukraine, and are simple and incomprehensible like the stories in the Bible. But are they not themselves stories of a new Bible?

When we arrived at the yard they took us to the *Eisenröhreplatz*, which is the levelling where they unload the iron pipes, and then the normal things of every day began. The Kapo made a second roll-call, briefly made note of the new acquisition and arranged with the civilian *Meister* about the day's work. He then entrusted us to the *Vorarbeiter* and went to sleep in the tool cabin, next to the stove; he is not a Kapo who makes trouble, for he is not a Jew and so has no fear of losing his post. The *Vorarbeiter* distributed the iron levers among us and the jacks among his friends. The usual little struggle took place to get the lightest levers, and today it went badly for me: mine is the twisted one which weighs perhaps thirty-five pounds; I know that even if I had to use it without any weight on it, I would be dead of exhaustion in half an hour.

Then we left, each with his own lever, limping in the melting snow. At every step a little snow and mud stuck to the wooden soles of our shoes, until one walked unsteadily on two heavy, formless masses of which it was impossible to free oneself; then, when one suddenly came unstuck, it felt as if one leg was a hand shorter than the other.

Today we have to unload an enormous, cast-iron cylinder from the wagon: I think it is a synthesis tube and will weigh several tons. This is better for us, as it is notoriously less exhausting to work with big loads than with small ones; in fact, the work is better subdivided, and we are given adequate tools. However, it is dangerous, one dare not let one's attention wander, a moment's oversight is sufficient to find oneself crushed.

Meister Nogalla, the Polish superintendent, rigid, serious and taciturn, supervised in person the unloading operation. Now the cylinder lies on the ground and Meister Nogalla says: '*Bohlen holen.*'

Our hearts sink. It means 'carry the sleepers' in order to build the path in the soft mud on which the cylinder will be pushed by lever into the factory. But the wooden sleepers are mortised in the ground and weigh about 175 pounds; they are more or less at the limits of our strength. The more robust of us, working in pairs, are able to carry sleepers for a few hours; for me it is a torture, the load maims my shoulder-bone. After the first journey I am deaf and almost blind from the effort, and I would stoop to any baseness to avoid the second journey.

I will try and place myself with Resnyk; he seems a good worker and being taller will support the greater part of the weight. I know that it is in the natural order of events that Resnyk refuse me with disdain and form a pair with another more robust individual; then I will ask to go to the latrine and I will remain there as long as possible, and afterwards I will try to hide, with the certainty of being immediately traced, mocked at and hit; but anything is better than this work.

Instead Resnyk accepts, and even more, lifts up the sleeper by himself and rests it on my right shoulder with care; then he lifts up the other end, stoops to place it on his left shoulder and we leave.

The sleeper is coated with snow and mud; at every step it knocks against my ear and the snow slides down my neck. After fifty steps I am at the limit of what a person is theoretically able to support: my knees bend, my shoulder aches as if pressed in a vice, my equilibrium is in danger. At every step I feel my shoes sucked away by the greedy mud, by this omnipresent Polish mud whose monotonous horror fills our days.

I bite deeply into my lips; we know well that to gain a small, extraneous pain serves as a stimulant to mobilise our last reserves of energy. The Kapos also know it: some of them beat us from pure bestiality and violence, but others beat us when we are under a load almost lovingly, accompanying the blows with exhortations, as cart-drivers do with willing horses.

When we reach the cylinder we unload the sleeper on the ground and I remain stiff, with empty eyes, open mouth and hanging arms, sunk in the ephemeral and negative ecstasy of the cessation of pain. In a twilight of exhaustion I wait for the push which will force me to begin work again, and I try to take advantage of every second of waiting to recuperate some energy.

But the push never comes: Resnyk touches my elbow, we return as slowly as possible to the sleepers. There the others are wandering around in pairs, all trying to delay as long as possible before submitting to the load.

'Allons, petit, attrape.' This sleeper is dry and a little lighter, but at the end of the second journey I go to the Vorarbeiter and ask to go to the latrine.

We have the advantage that our latrine is rather far; this permits us, once a day, a slightly longer absence than normal. Moreover, as it is also forbidden to go there alone, Wachsmann, the weakest and most clumsy of the Kommando, has been invested with the duty of Scheissbegleiter, 'toilet companion'; by virtue of this appointment, Wachsmann is responsible for any hypothetical (laughable hypothesis!) attempt to escape, and more realistically, for every delay.

As my request was accepted, I leave in the mud and the grey snow among the scraps of metal, escorted by the small Wachsmann. I never manage to reach an understanding with him, as we have no language in common; but his comrades tell me that he is a rabbi, in fact a Melamed, a person learned in the Torah, and even more, in his own village in Galicia, was famed as a healer and a thaumaturge. Nor am I far from believing it when I think that this thin, fragile and soft figure has managed to work for two years without falling ill and without dying, but on the contrary is lit up by an amazing vitality in actions and words and spends long evenings discussing Talmudic questions incomprehensibly in Yiddish and Hebrew with Mendi, who is a modernist rabbi.

The latrine is an oasis of peace. It is a provisional latrine which the Germans have not yet provided with the customary wooden partitions to separate the various divisions: '*Nur für Engländer*', '*Nur für Polen*', '*Nur für Ukrainische Frauen*', and so on, with, a little apart, '*Nur für Häftlinge*'. Inside, shoulder by shoulder, sit four hollow-faced Häftlinge; a bearded old Russian worker with the blue stripe OST on his left arm; a Polish boy, with a large white P on his back and chest; an English POW, with his face splendidly shaven and rosy and his khaki uniform neat, ironed and clean, except for a large KG (*Kriegsgefangener*) on his back. A fifth Häftling stands at the door patiently and monotonously asking every civilian who enters loosening his belt: '*Êtes-vous français?*'

When I return to work the lorries with the rations can be seen passing, which means it is ten o'clock. It is already a respectable hour, as the midday pause can be almost glimpsed in the fog of the remote future, allowing us to derive a little more strength from the expectation.

I do another two or three trips with Resnyk, searching attentively, even going to distant piles, to find lighter sleepers, but by now all the best ones have already been carried and only the other ones remain, repellent, with sharp corners, heavy with mud and ice, with metal plates nailed in to fix the rails.

When Franz comes to call Wachsmann to go and claim the ration, it means that it is already eleven o'clock and the morning has almost finished – no one thinks about the afternoon. Then the corvée returns at 11.30, and the standard interrogation begins: how much soup today, what quality, if we were given it from the top or the bottom of the vat; I force myself not to ask these questions, but I cannot help listening eagerly to the replies, sniffing at the smoke carried by the wind from the kitchen.

And at last, like a celestial meteor, superhuman and impersonal like a sign from heaven, the midday siren explodes, granting a brief respite to our anonymous and harmonious tiredness and hunger. And the usual things happen again: we all run to the hut, and we queue up with our bowls ready and we all have an animal hurry to swell our bellies with the warm stew, but no one wants to be first, as the first person receives the most liquid ration. As usual, the Kapo mocks and insults us for our voracity and takes care not to stir the pot, as the bottom belongs notoriously to him. Then comes the bliss (positive, from the belly) of the distension and warmth of the stomach and of the cabin around the noisy stove. The smokers, with miserly and reverent gestures, roll a thin cigarette, while everybody's clothes, humid with mud and snow, give out a dense smoke at the heat of the stove, with the smell of a kennel or of a sheepfold.

A tacit convention ordains that no one speak: within a minute everyone is sleeping, jammed elbow against elbow, falling suddenly forwards and recovering with a stiffening of the back. Behind the barely closed eyelids, dreams break out violently, the usual dreams. To be at home, in a wonderfully hot bath. To be at home, seated at a table. To be at home, and tell the story of this hopeless work of ours, of this never-ending hunger, of the slave's way of sleeping.

Then, in the heart of the vapours of our torpid digestions, a painful nucleus condenses, and jars us and grows until it crosses the threshold of the consciousness and takes away the joy of sleep. '*Es wird bald ein Uhr sein*': it is almost one o'clock. Like a rapid, voracious cancer, it kills our sleep and oppresses us with a foreboding anguish: we listen to the wind blowing outside, and to the light rustle of the snow against the window, '*es wird schnell ein Uhr sein*'. While everyone clings on to his sleep, so as not to allow it to abandon him, all senses are taut with the horror of the signal which is about to come, which is outside the door, which is here . . .

Here it is. A thud at the window: Meister Nogalla has thrown a snowball against the window-pane, and now stands stiffly outside, holding his watch with its face turned towards us. The Kapo gets up, stretches himself, and says quietly as one who does not doubt that he will be obeyed: '*Alles heraus*,' all out.

Oh, if one could only cry! Oh, if one could only affront the wind as we once used to, on equal terms, and not as we do here, like cringing dogs.

We are outside and everyone picks up his lever. Resnyk drops his head between his shoulders, pulls his beret over his ears and lifts his face up to the low grey sky where the inexorable snow whirls around: '*Si j'avey une chien, je ne le chasse pas dehors.*'

7 A Good Day

The conviction that life has a purpose is rooted in every fibre of man, it is a property of the human substance. Free men give many names to this purpose, and think and talk a lot about its nature. But for us the question is simpler.

Today, in this place, our only purpose is to reach the spring. At the moment we care about nothing else. Behind this aim there is not at the moment any other aim. In the morning while we wait endlessly lined up in the roll-call square for the time to leave for work, while every breath of wind penetrates our clothes and runs in violent shivers over our defenceless bodies, and everything is grey around us, and we are grey; in the morning, when it is still dark, we all look at the sky in the east to spot the first signs of a milder season, and the rising of the sun is commented on every day: today a little earlier than yesterday, today a little warmer than yesterday, in two months, in a month, the cold will call a truce and we will have one enemy less.

Today the sun rose bright and clear for the first time from the horizon of mud. It is a Polish sun, cold, white and distant, and only warms the skin, but when it dissolved the last mists a murmur ran through our colourless numbers, and when even I felt its luke-warmth through my clothes I understood how men can worship the sun.

'*Das Schlimmste ist vorüber,*' said Ziegler, turning his pointed shoulders to the sun: the worst is over. Next to us there is a group of Greeks, those admirable and terrible Jews of Salonica, tenacious, thieving, wise, ferocious and united, so determined to live, such pitiless opponents in the struggle for life; those Greeks who have conquered in the kitchens and in the yards, and whom even the Germans respect and the Poles fear. They are in their third year of camp, and nobody knows better than them what the camp means. They now stand closely in a circle, shoulder to shoulder, and sing one of their interminable chants.

Felicio the Greek knows me. '*L'année prochaine à la maison!*' he shouts at me, and adds: '*à la maison par la Cheminée!*' Felicio has been at Birkenau. And they continue to sing and beat their feet in time and grow drunk on songs.

When we finally left by the main entrance of the camp, the sun was quite high and the sky serene. At midday one could see the mountains; to the west, the steeple of Auschwitz (a steeple here!), and all around the barrage balloons. The smoke from the Buna lay still in the cold air, and a row of low hills could be seen, green with forests: and our hearts tighten because we all know that Birkenau is there, that our women finished there, and that soon we too will finish there; but we are not used to seeing it.

For the first time we are aware that on both sides of the road, even here, the meadows are green; because, without a sun, a meadow is as if it were not green.

The Buna is not: the Buna is desperately and essentially opaque and grey. This huge entanglement of iron, concrete, mud and smoke is the negation of beauty. Its roads and buildings are named like us, by numbers or letters, not by weird and sinister names. Within its bounds not a blade of grass grows, and the soil is impregnated with the poisonous saps of coal and petroleum, and the only things alive are machines and slaves – and the former are more alive than the latter.

The Buna is as large as a city; besides the managers and German technicians, forty thousand foreigners work there, and fifteen to twenty languages are spoken. All the foreigners live in different Lagers which surround the Buna: the Lager of the English prisoners of war, the Lager of the Ukrainian women, the Lager of the French volunteers and others we do not know. Our Lager (*Judenlager, Vernichtungslager, Kazett*) by itself provides ten thousand workers who come from all the nations of Europe. We are the slaves of the slaves, whom all can give orders to, and our name is the number which we carry tattooed on our arm and sewn on our jacket.

The Carbide Tower, which rises in the middle of Buna and the top of which is rarely visible in the fog, was built by us. Its bricks were called *Ziegel, briques, tegula, cegli, kamenny, mattoni, téglak*, and they were cemented by hate; hate and discord, like the Tower of Babel, and it is this that we call it: *Babelturm, Bobelturm*; and in it we hate the insane dream of grandeur of our masters, their contempt for God and men, for us men.

And today just as in the old fable, we all feel, and the Germans themselves feel, that a curse – not transcendent and divine, but inherent and historical – hangs over the insolent building based on the confusion of languages and erected in defiance of Heaven like a stone oath.

As will be told, the Buna factory, on which the Germans were busy for four years and for which countless of us suffered and died, never produced a pound of synthetic rubber.

But today the eternal puddles, on which a rainbow veil of petroleum trembles, reflect the serene sun. Pipes, rails, boilers, still cold from the freezing of the night, are dripping with dew. The earth dug up from the pits, the piles of coal, the blocks of concrete, exhale in light vapours the humidity of the winter.

Today is a good day. We look around like blind people who have recovered their sight, and we look at each other. We have never seen each other in sunlight: someone smiles. If it was not for the hunger!

For human nature is such that grief and pain – even simultane-ously suffered – do not add up as a whole in our consciousness, but hide, the lesser behind the greater, according to a definite law of perspective. It is providential and is our means of surviving in the camp. And this is the reason why so often in free life one hears it said that man is never content. In fact it is not a question of a human incapacity for a state of absolute happiness, but of an ever-insufficient knowledge of the complex nature of the state of unhappiness; so that the single name of the major cause is given to all its causes, which are composite and set out in an order of urgency. And if the most immediate cause of stress comes to an end, you are grievously amazed to see that another one lies behind; and in reality a whole series of others.

So that as soon as the cold, which throughout the winter had seemed our only enemy, had ceased, we became aware of our hunger; and repeating the same error, we now say: 'If it was not for the hunger! . . .'

But how could one imagine not being hungry? The Lager *is* hunger: we ourselves are hunger, living hunger.

On the other side of the road a steam-shovel is working. Its mouth, hanging from its cables, opens wide its steel jaws, balances a moment as if uncertain in its choice, then rushes upon the soft, clayey soil and snaps it up voraciously, while a satisfied snort of thick white smoke rises from the control cabin. Then it rises, turns half around, vomits backwards its mouthful and begins again.

Leaning on our shovels, we stop to watch, fascinated. At every bite of its mouth our mouths also open, our Adam's apples dance up and down, wretchedly visible under the flaccid skin. We are unable to tear ourselves away from the sight of the steam-shovel's meal.

Sigi is seventeen years old and is hungrier than everybody, although he is given a little soup every evening by his probably not disinterested protector. He had begun to speak of his home in Vienna and of his mother, but then he slipped on to the subject of food and now he talks endlessly about some wedding luncheon and remembers with genuine regret that he failed to finish his third plate of bean soup. And everyone tells him to keep quiet, but within ten minutes Béla is describing his Hungarian countryside and the fields of maize and a recipe to make meat pies with corn-cobs and lard and spices and . . . and he is cursed, sworn at and a third one begins to describe . . .

How weak our flesh is! I am perfectly well aware how vain these fantasies of hunger are, but dancing before my eyes I see the spaghetti which we had just cooked, Vanda, Luciana, Franco and I, at the sorting-camp when we suddenly heard the news that we would leave for here the following day; and we were eating it (it was so good, yellow, filling), and we stopped, fools, stupid as we were – if we had only known! And if it happened again . . . Absurd. If there is one thing sure in this world it is certainly this: that it will not happen to us a second time.

Fischer, the newest arrival, pulls out of his pocket a bundle, tied together with the painstaking exactitude of the Hungarians, and inside there is a half-ration of bread: half of this morning's bread. It is notorious that only the High Numbers keep their bread in their pockets; none of us old ones is able to preserve our bread for an hour. Various theories circulate to justify this incapacity of ours: bread eaten a little at a time is not wholly assimilated; the nervous tension needed to preserve the bread without touching it when one is hungry is in the highest degree harmful and debilitating; bread which is turning stale soon loses its alimentary value, so that the sooner it is eaten, the more nutritious it is; Alberto says that hunger

and bread in one's pocket are terms of opposite sign which automatically cancel each other out and cannot exist in the same
individual; and the majority affirm justly that, in the end, one's
stomach is the securest safe against thefts and extortions. '*Moi, on
m'a jamais volé mon pain!*' David snarls, hitting his concave stomach: but he is unable to take his eyes off Fischer who chews slowly
and methodically, 'lucky' enough to still have half a ration at ten in
the morning: '*Sacré veinard, va!*'

But it is not only because of the sun that today is a happy day: at
midday a surprise awaits us. Besides the normal morning ration,
we discover in the hut a wonderful pot of over eleven gallons, one
of those from the Factory Kitchen, almost full. Templer looks at us,
triumphant; this 'organisation' is his work.

Templer is the official organiser of the Kommando: he has an
astonishing nose for the soup of civilians, like bees for flowers. Our
Kapo, who is not a bad Kapo, leaves him a free hand, and with
reason: Templer slinks off, following imperceptible tracks like a
bloodhound, and returns with the priceless news that the Methanol
Polish workers, one mile from here, have abandoned ten gallons of
soup that tasted rancid, or that a wagonload of turnips is to be
found unguarded on the siding next to the Factory Kitchen.

Today there are ninety pints and we are fifteen, Kapo and *Vorarbeiter* included. This means six pints each: we will have two at
midday as well as the normal ration, and will come back to the hut
in turns for the other four during the afternoon, besides being
granted an extra five minutes' suspension of work to fill ourselves
up.

What more could one want? Even our work seems light, with
the prospect of four hot, dense pints waiting for us in the hut. The
Kapo comes to us periodically and calls: '*Wer hat noch zu fressen?*'

He does not say it from derision or to sneer, but because this way of eating on our feet, furiously, burning our mouths and throats, without time to breathe, really is '*fressen*', the way of eating of animals, and certainly not '*essen*', the human way of eating, seated in front of a table, religiously. '*Fressen*' is exactly the word, and is used currently among us.

Meister Nogalla watches and closes an eye at our absences from work. Meister Nogalla also has a hungry look about him, and if it were not for the social conventions, perhaps he would not despise a couple of pints of our warm broth.

Templer's turn comes. By plebiscitary consensus, he has been allowed ten pints, taken from the bottom of the pot. For Templer is not only a good organiser, but an exceptional soup-eater, and is uniquely able to empty his bowels at his own desire and in anticipation of a large meal, which contributes to his amazing gastric capacity.

Of this gift of his, he is justly proud, and everybody, even Meister Nogalla, knows about it. Accompanied by the gratitude of all, Templer the benefactor enters the latrine for a few moments and comes out beaming and ready, and amidst the general benevolence prepares to enjoy the fruits of his work: '*Nu, Templer, hast du Platz genug für die Suppe gemacht?*'

At sunset, the siren of the *Feierabend* sounds, the end of work; and as we are all satiated, at least for a few hours, no quarrels arise, we feel good, the Kapo feels no urge to hit us, and we are able to think of our mothers and wives, which usually does not happen. For a few hours we can be unhappy in the manner of free men.

8 This Side of Good and Evil

We had an incorrigible tendency to see a symbol and a sign in every event. For seventy days we had been waiting for the *Wäschetauschen*, the ceremony of the change of underclothes, and a rumour circulated persistently that the change of laundry had not taken place because, as the front had moved forward, the Germans were unable to gather together new transport at Auschwitz, and 'therefore' the liberation was near. And equally, the opposite interpretation circulated: that the delay in the change was a sure sign of an approaching integral liquidation of the camp. Instead the change took place, and as usual, the directors of the Lager took every care to make it occur unexpectedly and at the same time in all the huts.

It has to be realised that cloth is lacking in the Lager and is precious; and that our only way of acquiring a rag to blow our noses, or a pad for our shoes, is precisely that of cutting off the tail of a shirt at the time of the exchange. If the shirt has long sleeves, one cuts the sleeves; if not, one has to make do with a square from the bottom, or by unstitching one of the many patches. But in all cases a certain time is needed to get hold of needle and thread and to carry out the operation with some skill, so as not to leave the damage too obvious at the time of handing it in. The dirty, tattered washing is passed on, thrown together, to the tailor's workshop in the camp, where it is summarily pieced up, sent to the steam disinfection (not washed!) and is then redistributed; hence the need to make the exchanges as unexpected as possible, so as to save the soiled washing from the above mutilations.

But, as always happens, it was not possible to prevent a cunning glance piercing through the canvas of the cart which was leaving after the disinfection, so that within a few minutes the camp knew of the imminence of a *Wäschetauschen*, and in addition, that this time there were new shirts from a convoy of Hungarians which had arrived three days ago.

The news had immediate repercussions. All who illegally possessed second shirts, stolen or organised, or even honestly bought with bread as a protection against the cold or to invest capital in a moment of prosperity, immediately rushed to the Exchange Market, hoping to arrive in time to barter their reserve shirts for food products before the flood of new shirts, or the certainty of their arrival, irreparably devalued the price of the article.

The Market is always very active. Although every exchange (in fact, every form of possession) is explicitly forbidden, and although frequent swoops of Kapos or *Blockältester* sent merchants, customers and the curious periodically flying, nevertheless, the north-east corner of the Lager (significantly the corner furthest from the SS huts) is permanently occupied by a tumultuous throng, in the open during the summer, in a washroom during the winter, as soon as the squads return from work.

Here scores of prisoners driven desperate by hunger prowl around, with lips half open and eyes gleaming, lured by a deceptive instinct to where the merchandise shown makes the gnawing of their stomachs more acute and their salvation more arduous. In the best cases they possess a miserable half-ration of bread which, with painful effort, they have saved since the morning, in the senseless hope of a chance to make an advantageous bargain with some ingenuous person, unaware of the prices of the moment. Some of these, with savage patience, acquire with their half-ration two pints of soup which, once in their possession, they subject to a methodical examination with a view to extracting the few pieces of potato lying at the bottom; this done, they exchange it for bread, and the bread for another two pints to denaturalise, and so on until their nerves are exhausted, or until some victim, catching them in the act, inflicts on them a severe lesson, exposing them to public derision. Of the same kind are those who come to the Market to sell their only shirt; they well know what will happen on the next occasion that the Kapo finds out that they are bare underneath their jackets. The Kapo will ask them what they have done with their shirt; it is a purely rhetorical question, a formality useful only to begin the game. They will reply that their shirt was stolen in the washroom; this reply is equally customary, and is not expected to be believed; in fact, even the stones of the Lager know that ninety-nine times out of a hundred whoever has no shirt has sold it because of hunger, and that in any case one is responsible for one's shirt because it belongs to the Lager. Then the Kapo will beat them, they will be issued another shirt, and sooner or later they will begin again.

The professional merchants stand in the Market, each one in his normal corner; first among them come the Greeks, as immobile and silent as sphinxes, squatting on the ground behind their bowls of thick soup, the fruits of their labour, of their co-operation and of their national solidarity. The Greeks have been reduced to very few by now, but they have made a contribution of the first importance to the physiognomy of the camp and to the international slang in circulation. Everyone knows that 'caravana' is the bowl, and that 'la comedera es buena' means that the soup is good; the word that expresses the generic idea of theft is 'klepsiklepsi', of obvious Greek origin. These few survivors from the Jewish colony of Salonica, with their two languages, Spanish and Greek, and their numerous activities, are the repositories of a concrete, mundane, conscious wisdom, in which the traditions of all the Mediterranean civilisations blend together. That this wisdom was transformed in the camp into the systematic and scientific practice of theft and seizure of positions and the monopoly of the bargaining Market, should not let one forget that their aversion to gratuitous brutality, their amazing consciousness of the survival of at least a potential human dignity, made of the Greeks the most coherent national nucleus in Lager, and in this respect, the most civilised.

At the Market you can find specialists in kitchen thefts, their jackets swollen with strange bulges. While there is a virtually stable price for soup (half a ration of bread for two pints), the quotations for turnips, carrots and potatoes are extremely variable and depend greatly, among other factors, on the diligence and the corruptibility of the guards at the stores.

Mahorca is sold. Mahorca is a third-rate tobacco, crude and wooden, which is officially on sale at the canteen in one-and-a-half-ounce packets, in exchange for the prize-coupons that the Buna ought to distribute to the best workers. Such a distribution occurs irregularly, with great parsimony and open injustice, so that the greatest number of the coupons end up, either legitimately or through abuse of authority, in the hands of the Kapos and of the Prominents; nevertheless the prize-coupons still circulate on the Market in the form of money, and their value changes in strict obedience to the laws of classical economics.

There have been periods in which the prize-coupon was worth one ration of bread, then one-and-a-quarter, even one-and-a-third; one day it was quoted at one-and-a-half ration, but then the supply of Mahorca to the canteen failed, so that, lacking a cover, the money collapsed at once to a quarter of a ration. Another boom period occurred for a singular reason: the arrival of a fresh contingent of robust Polish girls in place of the old inmates of the Frauenblock. In fact, as the prize-coupon is valid for entry to the Frauenblock (for the criminals and the politicals; not for the Jews, who, on the other hand, do not feel affected by this restriction), those interested actively and rapidly cornered the market: hence the revaluation, which, in any case, did not last long.

Among the ordinary Häftlinge there are not many who search for Mahorca to smoke it personally; for the most part it leaves the camp and ends in the hands of the civilian workers of the Buna. The traffic is an instance of a kind of '*kombinacja*' frequently practised: the Häftling, somehow saving a ration of bread, invests it in Mahorca; he cautiously gets in touch with a civilian addict who acquires the Mahorca, paying in cash with a portion of bread greater than that initially invested. The Häftling eats the surplus, and puts back on the market the remaining ration. Speculations of this kind establish a tie between the internal economy of the Lager and the economic life of the outside world: the accidental failure of the distribution of tobacco among the civilian population of Cracow, overcoming the barrier of barbed wire which segregates us from human society, had an immediate repercussion in camp, provoking a notable rise in the quotation of Mahorca, and consequently of the prize-coupon.

The process outlined above is no more than the most simple of examples: another more complex one is the following. The Häftling acquires in exchange for Mahorca or bread, or even obtains as a gift from a civilian, some abominable, ragged, dirty shred of a shirt, which must however have three holes suitable to fit more or less over the head and arms. So long as it only carries signs of wear, and not of artificially created mutilations, such an object, at the time of the *Wäschetauschen*, is valid as a shirt and carries the right of an exchange; at the most, the person who presents it will receive an adequate measure of blows for having taken so little care of camp clothing.

Consequently, within the Lager, there is no great difference in value between a shirt worthy of the name and a tattered thing full of patches; the Häftling described above will have no difficulty in finding a comrade in possession of a shirt of commercial value who is unable to capitalise on it as he is not in touch with civilian workers, either because of his place of work, or through difficulties of language or intrinsic incapacity. This latter will be satisfied with a modest amount of bread for the exchange, and in fact the next *Wäschetauschen* will to a certain extent re-establish equilibrium, distributing good and bad washing in a perfectly casual manner. But the first Häftling will be able to smuggle the good shirt into Buna and sell it to the original civilian (or to any other) for four, six, even ten rations of bread. This high margin of profit is correlative to the gravity of the risk of leaving camp wearing more than one shirt or re-entering with none.

There are many variations on this theme. There are some who do not hesitate to have the gold fillings of their teeth extracted to sell them in Buna for bread or tobacco. But the most common of cases is that such traffic takes place through an intermediary. A High Number, that is, a new arrival, only recently but sufficiently besotted by hunger and by the extreme tension of life in the camp, is noticed by a Low Number for the number of his gold teeth; the Low offers the High three or four rations of bread to be paid in return for extraction. If the High Number accepts, the Low one pays, carries the gold to Buna, and if in contact with a civilian of trust, from whom he fears neither denunciation nor fraudulent dealing, he can make a gain of ten or even as much as twenty or more rations, which are paid to him gradually, one or two a day. It is worth noting in this respect that contrary to what takes place in Buna, the maximum total of any transaction negotiated *within* the camp is four rations of bread, because it would be practically impossible either to make contracts on credit, or to preserve a larger quantity of bread from the greed of others or one's own hunger.

Traffic with civilians is a characteristic element of the *Arbeitslager*, and as we have seen, determines its economic life. On the other hand, it is a crime, explicitly foreseen by the camp regulations, and considered equivalent to 'political' crimes; so that it is punished with particular severity. The Häftling convicted of '*Handel mit Zivilisten*', unless he can rely on powerful influences, ends up at Gleiwitz III, at Janina or at Heidebreck in the coalmines; which means death from exhaustion in the course of a few weeks. Moreover, his accomplice, the civilian worker, may also be denounced to the competent German authority and condemned to pass a period in *Vernichtungslager*, under the same conditions as us; a period varying, as far as I can see, from a fortnight to eight months. The workmen who experience this retaliation have their possessions taken away like us on their entry, but their personal effects are kept in a special storeroom. They are not tattooed and they keep their hair, which makes them easily recognisable, but for the whole duration of the punishment they are subjected to the same work and the same discipline as us – except, of course, the selections.

They work in separate Kommandos and they have no contact of any sort with the common Häftlinge. In fact, the Lager is for them a punishment, and if they do not die of exhaustion or illness they can expect to return among men; if they could communicate with us, it would create a breach in the wall which keeps us dead to the world, and a ray of light into the mystery which prevails among free men about our condition. For us, on the contrary, the Lager is not a punishment; for us, no end is foreseen and the Lager is nothing but a manner of living assigned to us, without limits of time, in the bosom of the Germanic social organism.

One section of the camp itself is in fact set aside for civilian workers of all nationalities who are compelled to stay there for a longer or shorter period in expiation of their illicit relations with Häftlinge. This section is separated from the rest of the camp by barbed wire, and is called E-Lager, and its guests E-Häftlinge. 'E' is the initial for 'Erziehung' which means education.

All the bargaining transactions outlined above are based on the smuggling of materials belonging to the Lager. This is why the SS are so eager to suppress them: the very gold of our teeth is their property, as sooner or later, torn from the mouths of the living or the dead, it ends up in their hands. So it is natural that they should take care that the gold does not leave the camp.

But against theft in itself, the direction of the camp has no prejudice. The attitude of open connivance by the SS as regards smuggling in the opposite direction shows this clearly.

Here things are generally more simple. It is a question of stealing or receiving any of the various tools, utensils, materials, products, etc. with which we come in daily contact in Buna in the course of our work, of introducing them into the camp in the evening, of finding a customer and of effecting the exchange for bread or soup. This traffic is intense: for certain articles, although they are necessary for the normal life of the Lager, this method of theft in Buna is the only and regular way of provisioning. Typical are the instances of brooms, paint, electric wire, grease for shoes. The traffic in this last item will serve as an example.

As we have stated elsewhere, the camp regulations prescribe the greasing and polishing of shoes every morning, and every Block-ältester is responsible to the SS for obedience to this order by all the men in his hut. One would think that each hut would enjoy a periodic assignment of grease for shoes, but this is not so; the mechanism is completely different. It needs to be stated first that each hut receives an assignment of soup somewhat higher than that prescribed for regulation rations; the extra is divided according to the discretion of the *Blockältester*, who first of all distributes the gifts to his friends and protégés, then the recompense to the hut-sweepers, to the night guards, to the lice-controllers and to all other Prominents and functionaries in the hut. What is still left over (and every smart *Blockältester* makes sure that there is always some over) is used precisely for these acquisitions.

The rest is obvious. Those Häftlinge at Buna who have the chance to fill their bowl with grease or machine-oil (or anything else: any blackish and greasy substance is considered suitable for the purpose), on their return to the camp in the evening, make a systematic tour of the huts until they find a *Blockältester* who has run out of the article and wants a fresh supply. In addition, every hut usually has its habitual supplier, who has been allotted a fixed daily recompense on condition that he provides the grease every time that the reserve is about to run out.

Every evening, beside the doors of the *Tagesräume*, the groups of suppliers stand patiently around; on their feet for hours and hours in the rain or snow, they discuss excitedly matters relating to the fluctuation of prices and value of the prize-coupon. Every now and again one of them leaves the group, makes a quick visit to the Market and returns with the latest news.

Besides the articles already described, there are innumerable others to be found in Buna, which might be useful to the Block or welcomed by the *Blockältester*, or might excite the interest or curiosity of the Prominents: light-bulbs, ordinary or shaving-soap, files, pliers, sacks, nails; methylic alcohol is sold to make drinks; while petrol is useful for the rudimentary lighters, prodigies of the secret industry of the Lager craftsmen.

In this complex network of thefts and counter-thefts, nourished by the silent hostility between the SS command and the civilian authorities of the Buna, Ka-Be plays a part of prime importance. Ka-Be is the place of least resistance, where the regulations can most easily be avoided and the surveillance of the Kapos eluded. Everyone knows that it is the nurses themselves who send back on the market, at low prices, the clothes and shoes of the dead and of the selected who leave naked for Birkenau; it is the nurses and doctors who export the restricted sulphonamides to Buna, selling them to civilians for articles of food.

The nurses also make huge profits from the trade in spoons. The Lager does not provide the new arrivals with spoons, although the semi-liquid soup cannot be consumed without them. The spoons are manufactured in Buna, secretly and in their spare moments, by Häftlinge who work as Specialists in the iron- and tinsmith Kommandos: they are rough and clumsy tools, shaped from iron-plate worked by hammer, often with a sharp handle-edge to serve at the same time as a knife to cut the bread. The manufacturers themselves sell them directly to the new arrivals: an ordinary spoon is worth half a ration, a knife-spoon three-quarters of a ration of bread. Now it is a law that although one can enter Ka-Be with one's spoon, one cannot leave with it. At the moment of release, before the clothes are given, the healthy patient's spoon is confiscated by the nurses and placed on sale in the Market. Adding the spoons of the patients about to leave to those of the dead and selected, the nurses receive the gains of the sale of about fifty spoons every day. On the other hand, the dismissed patients are forced to begin work again with the initial disadvantage of half a ration of bread, set aside to acquire a new spoon.

Finally, Ka-Be is the main customer and receiver of thefts occurring in Buna: of the soup assigned to Ka-Be, a good forty pints are set aside every day as the theft-fund to acquire the most varied of goods from the Specialists. There are those who steal thin rubber tubing which is used in Ka-Be for enemas and for stomach-tubes; others offer coloured pencils and inks, necessary for Ka-Be's complicated book-keeping system; and thermometers and glass instruments and chemicals, which come from the Buna stores in the Häftlinge's pockets and are used in the infirmary as sanitary equipment.

And I would not like to be accused of immodesty if I add that it was our idea, mine and Alberto's, to steal the rolls of graph-paper from the thermographs of the Desiccation Department, and offer them to the Medical Chief of Ka-Be with the suggestion that they be used as paper for pulse–temperature charts.

In conclusion: theft in Buna, punished by the civil direction, is authorised and encouraged by the SS; theft in camp, severely repressed by the SS, is considered by the civilians as a normal exchange operation; theft among Häftlinge is generally punished, but the punishment strikes the thief and the victim with equal gravity. We now invite the reader to contemplate the possible meaning in the Lager of the words 'good' and 'evil', 'just' and 'unjust'; let everybody judge, on the basis of the picture we have outlined and of the examples given above, how much of our ordinary moral world could survive on this side of the barbed wire.

9 The Drowned and the Saved

What we have so far said and will say concerns the ambiguous life of the Lager. In our time many men have lived in this cruel manner, crushed against the bottom, but each for a relatively short period; so that we can perhaps ask ourselves if it is necessary or good to retain any memory of this exceptional human state.

To this question we feel that we have to reply in the affirmative. We are in fact convinced that no human experience is without meaning or unworthy of analysis, and that fundamental values, even if they are not positive, can be deduced from this particular world which we are describing. We would also like to consider that the Lager was pre-eminently a gigantic biological and social experiment.

Thousands of individuals, differing in age, condition, origin, language, culture and customs, are enclosed within barbed wire: there they live a regular, controlled life which is identical for all and inadequate to all needs, and which is more rigorous than any experimenter could have set up to establish what is essential and what adventitious to the conduct of the human animal in the struggle for life.

We do not believe in the most obvious and facile deduction: that man is fundamentally brutal, egoistic and stupid in his conduct once every civilised institution is taken away, and that the Häftling is consequently nothing but a man without inhibitions. We believe, rather, that the only conclusion to be drawn is that in the face of driving necessity and physical disabilities many social habits and instincts are reduced to silence.

But another fact seems to us worthy of attention: there comes to light the existence of two particularly well-differentiated categories among men – the saved and the drowned. Other pairs of opposites (the good and the bad, the wise and the foolish, the cowards and the courageous, the unlucky and the fortunate) are considerably less distinct, they seem less essential, and above all they allow for more numerous and complex intermediary gradations.

This division is much less evident in ordinary life; for there it rarely happens that a man loses himself. A man is normally not alone, and in his rise or fall is tied to the destinies of his neighbours; so that it is exceptional for anyone to acquire unlimited power, or to fall by a succession of defeats into utter ruin. Moreover, everyone is normally in possession of such spiritual, physical and even financial resources that the probabilities of a shipwreck, of total inadequacy in the face of life, are relatively small. And one must take into account a definite cushioning effect exercised both by the law, and by the moral sense which constitutes a self-imposed law; for a country is considered the more civilised the more the wisdom and efficiency of its laws hinder a weak man from becoming too weak or a powerful one too powerful.

But in the Lager things are different: here the struggle to survive is without respite, because everyone is desperately and ferociously alone. If some Null Achtzehn vacillates, he will find no one to extend a helping hand; on the contrary, someone will knock him aside, because it is in no one's interest that there will be one more 'musselman'* dragging himself to work every day; and if someone, by a miracle of savage patience and cunning, finds a new method of avoiding the hardest work, a new art which yields him an ounce of bread, he will try to keep his method secret, and he will be esteemed and respected for this, and will derive from it an exclusive, personal

* This word '*Muselmann*', I do not know why, was used by the old ones of the camp to describe the weak, the inept, those doomed to selection.

benefit; he will become stronger and so will be feared, and who is feared is, *ipso facto*, a candidate for survival.

In history and in life one sometimes seems to glimpse a ferocious law which states: 'to him that has, will be given; from him that has not, will be taken away'. In the Lager, where man is alone and where the struggle for life is reduced to its primordial mechanism, this unjust law is openly in force, is recognised by all. With the adaptable, the strong and astute individuals, even the leaders willingly keep contact, sometimes even friendly contact, because they hope later to perhaps derive some benefit. But with the musselmans, the men in decay, it is not even worth speaking, because one knows already that they will complain and will speak about what they used to eat at home. Even less worthwhile is it to make friends with them, because they have no distinguished acquaintances in camp, they do not gain any extra rations, they do not work in profitable Kommandos and they know no secret method of organising. And in any case, one knows that they are only here on a visit, that in a few weeks nothing will remain of them but a handful of ashes in some nearby field and a crossed-out number on a register. Although engulfed and swept along without rest by the innumerable crowd of those similar to them, they suffer and drag themselves along in an opaque intimate solitude, and in solitude they die or disappear, without leaving a trace in anyone's memory.

The result of this pitiless process of natural selection could be read in the statistics of Lager population movements. At Auschwitz, in 1944, of the old Jewish prisoners (we will not speak of the others here, as their condition was different), '*kleine Nummer*', Low Numbers less than 150,000, only a few hundred had survived; not one was an ordinary Häftling, vegetating in the ordinary Kommandos, and subsisting on the normal ration. There remained only the doctors, tailors, shoemakers, musicians, cooks, young attractive homosexuals, friends or compatriots of some authority in the camp; or they were particularly pitiless, vigorous and inhuman individuals, installed (following an investiture by the SS command, which showed itself in such choices to possess satanic knowledge of human beings) in the posts of Kapos, *Blockältester*, etc.; or finally, those who, without fulfilling particular functions, had always succeeded through their astuteness and energy in successfully organising, gaining in this way, besides material advantages and reputation, the indulgence and esteem of the powerful people in the camp. Whosoever does not know how to become an '*Organisator*', '*Kombinator*', '*Prominent*' (the savage eloquence of these words!), soon becomes a musselman. In life, a third way exists, and is in fact the rule; it does not exist in the concentration camp.

To sink is the easiest of matters; it is enough to carry out all the orders one receives, to eat only the ration, to observe the discipline of the work and the camp. Experience showed that only exceptionally could one survive more than three months in this way. All the musselmans who finished in the gas chambers have the same story, or more exactly, have no story; they followed the slope down to the bottom, like streams that run down to the sea. On their entry into the camp, through basic incapacity, or by misfortune, or through some banal incident, they are overcome before they can adapt themselves; they are beaten by time, they do not begin to learn German, to disentangle the infernal knot of laws and prohibitions until their body is already in decay, and nothing can save them from selections or from death by exhaustion. Their life is short, but their number is endless; they, the *Muselmänner*, the drowned, form the backbone of the camp, an anonymous mass, continually renewed and always identical, of non-men who march and labour in silence, the divine spark dead within them, already too empty to really suffer. One hesitates to call them living: one hesitates to call their death death, in the face of which they have no fear, as they are too tired to understand.

They crowd my memory with their faceless presences, and if I could enclose all the evil of our time in one image, I would choose this image which is familiar to me: an emaciated man, with head dropped and shoulders curved, on whose face and in whose eyes not a trace of a thought is to be seen.

If the drowned have no story, and single and broad is the path to perdition, the paths to salvation are many, difficult and improbable.

The most travelled road, as we have stated, is that of the '*Prominent*'. '*Prominenten*' is the name for the camp officials, from the Häftling-director (*Lagerältester*) to the Kapos, the cooks, the nurses, the night guards, even to the hut-sweepers and to the *Scheissminister* and *Bademeister* (superintendents of the latrines and showers). We are more particularly interested in the Jewish Prominents, because while the others are automatically invested with offices as they enter the camp in virtue of their natural supremacy, the Jews have to plot and struggle hard to gain them.

The Jewish Prominents form a sad and notable human phenomenon. In them converge present, past and atavistic sufferings, and the tradition of hostility towards the stranger makes of them monsters of asociality and insensitivity.

They are the typical product of the structure of the German Lager: if one offers a position of privilege to a few individuals in a state of slavery, exacting in exchange the betrayal of a natural solidarity with their comrades, there will certainly be someone who will accept. He will be withdrawn from the common law and will become untouchable; the more power that he is given, the more he will be consequently hateful and hated. When he is given the command of a group of unfortunates, with the right of life or death

over them, he will be cruel and tyrannical, because he will understand that if he is not sufficiently so, someone else, judged more
suitable, will take over his post. Moreover, his capacity for hatred,
unfulfilled in the direction of the oppressors, will double back,
beyond all reason, on the oppressed; and he will only be satisfied
when he has unloaded on to his underlings the injury received
from above.

We are aware that this is very distant from the picture that is
usually given of the oppressed who unite, if not in resistance, at
least in suffering. We do not deny that this may be possible when
oppression does not pass a certain limit, or perhaps when the
oppressor, through inexperience or magnanimity, tolerates or
favours it. But we state that in our days, in all countries in which a
foreign people have set foot as invaders, an analogous position of
rivalry and hatred among the subjected has been brought about;
and this, like many other human characteristics, could be experienced in the Lager in the light of particularly cruel evidence.

About the non-Jewish Prominents there is less to say, although
they were far and away the most numerous (no 'Aryan' Häftling
was without a post, however modest). That they were stolid and
bestial is natural when one thinks that the majority were ordinary
criminals, chosen from the German prisons for the very purpose of
their employment as superintendents of the camps for Jews; and
we maintain that it was a very apt choice, because we refuse to
believe that the squalid human specimens whom we saw at work
were an average example, not of Germans in general, but even of
German prisoners in particular. It is difficult to explain how in
Auschwitz the political German, Polish and Russian Prominents
rivalled the ordinary convicts in brutality. But it is known that in
Germany the qualification of political crime also applied to such
acts as clandestine trade, illicit relations with Jewish women, theft

from Party officials. The 'real' politicals lived and died in other camps, with names now sadly famous, in notoriously hard conditions, which, however, in many aspects differed from those described here.

But besides the officials in the strict sense of the word, there is a vast category of prisoners, not initially favoured by fate, who fight merely with their own strength to survive. One has to fight against the current; to battle every day and every hour against exhaustion, hunger, cold and the resulting inertia; to resist enemies and have no pity for rivals; to sharpen one's wits, build up one's patience, strengthen one's will-power. Or else, to throttle all dignity and kill all conscience, to climb down into the arena as a beast against other beasts, to let oneself be guided by those unsuspected subterranean forces which sustain families and individuals in cruel times. Many were the ways devised and put into effect by us in order not to die: as many as there are different human characters. All implied a weakening struggle of one against all, and a by no means small sum of aberrations and compromises. Survival without renunciation of any part of one's own moral world – apart from powerful and direct interventions by fortune – was conceded only to very few superior individuals, made of the stuff of martyrs and saints.

We will try to show in how many ways it was possible to reach salvation with the stories of Schepschel, Alfred L., Elias and Henri.

Schepschel has been living in the Lager for four years. He has seen the death of tens of thousands of those like him, beginning with the pogrom which had driven him from his village in Galicia. He had a wife and five children and a prosperous business as a saddler, but for a long time now he has grown accustomed to thinking of himself only as a sack which needs periodic refilling. Schepschel is not very robust, nor very courageous, nor very wicked; he is not even particularly astute, nor has he ever found a method which allows him a little respite, but he is reduced to small and occasional expedients, '*kombinacje*' as they are called here.

Every now and again he steals a broom in Buna and sells it to the *Blockältester*; when he manages to set aside a little bread-capital, he hires the tools of the cobbler in the Block, his compatriot, and works on his own account for a few hours; he knows how to make braces with interlaced electric wires. Sigi told me that he has seen him during the midday interval singing and dancing in front of the hut of the Slovak workers, who sometimes reward him with the remainders of their soup.

This said, one would be inclined to think of Schepschel with indulgent sympathy, as of a poor wretch who retains only a humble and elementary desire to live, and who bravely carries on his small struggle not to give way. But Schepschel was no exception, and when the opportunity showed itself, he did not hesitate to have Moischl, his accomplice in a theft from the kitchen, condemned to a flogging, in the mistaken hope of gaining favour in the eyes of the *Blockältester* and furthering his candidature for the position of *Kesselwäscher*, 'vat-washer'.

The story of engineer Alfred L. shows among other things how vain is the myth of original equality among men.

In his own country L. was the director of an extremely important factory of chemical products, and his name was (and is) well known in industrial circles throughout Europe. He was a robust man of about fifty; I do not know how he had been arrested, but he entered the camp like all others: naked, alone and unknown. When I knew him he was very wasted away, but still showed on his face the signs of a disciplined and methodical energy; at that time, his privileges were limited to the daily cleaning of the Polish workers' pots; this work, which he had gained in some manner as his exclusive monopoly, yielded him half a ladleful of soup per day. Certainly it was not enough to satisfy his hunger; nevertheless, no one had ever heard him complain. In fact, the few words that he let slip implied imposing secret resources, a solid and fruitful 'organisation'.

This was confirmed by his appearance. L. had a 'line': with his hands and face always perfectly clean, he had the rare self-denial to wash his shirt every fortnight, without waiting for the bi-monthly change (we would like to point out here that to wash a shirt meant finding soap, time and space in the overcrowded washroom; adapting oneself to keep watch carefully on the wet shirt without losing attention for a moment, and to put it on, naturally still wet, in the silence-hour when the lights are turned out); he owned a pair of wooden shoes to go to the shower, and even his striped suit was singularly adapted to his appearance, clean and new. L. had acquired in practice the whole appearance of a Prominent considerably before becoming one; only a long time after did I find out that L. was able to earn all this show of prosperity with incredible tenacity, paying for his individual acquisitions and services with bread from his own ration, so imposing upon himself a regime of supplementary privations.

His plan was a long-term one, which is all the more notable as conceived in an environment dominated by a mentality of the provisional; and L. carried it out with rigid inner discipline, without pity for himself or – with greater reason – for comrades who crossed his path. L. knew that the step was short from being judged powerful to effectively becoming so, and that everywhere, and especially in the midst of the general levelling of the Lager, a respectable appearance is the best guarantee of being respected. He took every care not to be confused with the mass; he worked with stubborn duty, even occasionally admonishing his lazy comrades in a persuasive and deprecatory tone of voice; he avoided the daily struggle for the best place in the queue for the ration, and prepared to take the first ration, notoriously the most liquid, every day, so as to be noticed by his *Blockältester* for his discipline. To complete the separation, he always behaved in his relations with his comrades with the maximum courtesy compatible with his egotism, which was absolute.

When the Chemical Kommando was formed, as will be described, L. knew that his hour had struck: he needed no more than his spruce suit and his emaciated and shaved face in the midst of the flock of his sordid and slovenly colleagues to at once convince both Kapo and *Arbeitsdienst* that he was one of the genuinely saved, a potential Prominent; so that (to him who has, shall be given) he was without hesitation appointed Specialist, nominated technical head of the Kommando, and taken on by the Direction of the Buna as analyst in the laboratory of the styrene department. He was subsequently appointed to examine all the new intake to the Chemical Kommando, to judge their professional ability; which he always did with extreme severity, especially when faced with those in whom he smelled possible future rivals.

I do not know how his story continued; but I feel it is quite probable that he managed to escape death, and today is still living his cold life of the determined and joyless dominator.

Elias Lindzin, 141565, one day tumbled into the Chemical Kommando. He was a dwarf, not more than five feet high, but I have never seen muscles like his. When he is naked you can see every muscle taut under his skin, like a poised animal; his body, enlarged without alteration of proportions, would serve as a good model for a Hercules: but you must not look at his head.

Under his scalp, the skull sutures stand out immoderately. The cranium is massive and gives the impression of being made of metal or stone; the limit of his shaven hair shows up barely a finger's width above his eyebrows. The nose, the chin, the forehead, the cheekbones are hard and compact, the whole face looks like a battering-ram, an instrument made for butting. A sense of bestial vigour emanates from his body.

To see Elias work is a disconcerting spectacle; the Polish Meister, even the Germans sometimes stop to admire Elias at work. Nothing seems impossible to him. While we barely carry one sack of cement, Elias carries two, then three, then four, keeping them balanced no one knows how, and while he hurries along on his short, squat legs, he makes faces under the load, he laughs, curses, shouts and sings without pause, as if he had lungs made of bronze. Despite his wooden shoes Elias climbs like a monkey on to the scaffolding and runs safely on cross-beams poised over nothing; he carries six bricks at a time balanced on his head; he knows how to make a spoon from a piece of tin, and a knife from a scrap of steel; he finds dry paper, wood and coal everywhere and knows how to start a fire in a few moments even in the rain. He is a tailor, a carpenter, a cobbler, a barber; he can spit incredible distances; he sings, in a not unpleasant bass voice, Polish and Yiddish songs never heard before; he can ingest ten, fifteen, twenty pints of soup without vomiting and without having diarrhoea, and begin work again immediately after. He knows how to make a big hump come out between his shoulders, and goes around the hut, bow-legged and mimicking, shouting and declaiming incomprehensibly, to the joy of the Prominents of the camp. I saw him fight a Pole a whole head taller than him and knock him down with a blow of his cranium into the stomach, as powerful and accurate as a catapult. I never saw him rest, I never saw him quiet or still, I never saw him injured or ill.

Of his life as a free man, no one knows anything; and in any case, to imagine Elias as a free man requires a great effort of fantasy and induction; he only speaks Polish, and the surly and deformed Yiddish of Warsaw; besides it is impossible to keep him to a coherent conversation. He might be twenty or forty years old; he usually says that he is thirty-three, and that he has begot seventeen children – which is not unlikely. He talks continuously on the most varied of subjects; always in a resounding voice, in an oratorical manner, with the violent mimicry of the deranged; as if he was always talking to a dense crowd – and as is natural, he never lacks an audience. Those who understand his language drink up his declamations, shaking with laughter; they pat him enthusiastically on the back – a back as hard as iron – inciting him to continue; while he, fierce and frowning, whirls around like a wild animal in the circle of his spectators, apostrophizing now one, now another of them; he suddenly grabs hold of one by the chest with his small hooked paw, irresistibly drags him to himself, vomits into his face an incomprehensible invective, then throws him back like a piece of wood, and amidst the applause and laughter, with his arms reaching up to the heavens like some little prophetic monster, continues his raging and crazy speech.

His fame as an exceptional worker spread quite soon, and by the absurd law of the Lager, from then on he practically ceased to work. His help was requested directly by the Meister only for such work as required skill and special vigour. Apart from these services he insolently and violently supervised our daily, flat exhaustion, frequently disappearing on mysterious visits and adventures in who knows what recesses of the yard, from which he returned with large bulges in his pockets and often with his stomach visibly full.

Elias is naturally and innocently a thief: in this he shows the instinctive astuteness of wild animals. He is never caught in the act because he only steals when there is a good chance; but when this chance comes Elias steals as fatally and foreseeably as a stone drops. Apart from the fact that it is difficult to surprise him, it is obvious that it would be of no use punishing him for his thefts: to him they imply a vital act like breathing or sleeping.

We can now ask who is this man Elias. If he is a madman, incomprehensible and para-human, who ended in the Lager by chance. If he is an atavism, different from our modern world, and better adapted to the primordial conditions of camp life. Or if he is perhaps a product of the camp itself, what we will all become if we do not die in the camp, and if the camp itself does not end first.

There is some truth in all three suppositions. Elias has survived the destruction from outside, because he is physically indestructible; he has resisted the annihilation from within because he is insane. So, in the first place, he is a survivor: he is the most adaptable, the human type most suited to this way of living.

If Elias regains his liberty he will be confined to the fringes of human society, in a prison or a lunatic asylum. But here in the Lager there are no criminals nor madmen; no criminals because there is no moral law to contravene, no madmen because we are wholly devoid of free will, as our every action is, in time and place, the only conceivable one.

In the Lager Elias prospers and is triumphant. He is a good worker and a good organiser, and for this double reason, he is safe from selections and respected by both leaders and comrades. For those who have no sound inner resources, for those who do not know how to draw from their own consciences sufficient force to cling to life, the only road to salvation leads to Elias: to insanity and to deceitful bestiality. All the other roads are dead ends.

This said, one might perhaps be tempted to draw conclusions, and perhaps even rules for our daily life. Are there not all around us some Eliases, more or less in embryo? Do we not see individuals living without purpose, lacking all forms of self-control and conscience, who live not *in spite of* these defects, but like Elias precisely because of them?

The question is serious, but will not be further discussed as we want these to be stories of the Lager, while much has already been written on man outside the Lager. But one thing we would like to add: Elias, as far as we could judge from outside, and as far as the phrase can have meaning, was probably a happy person.

Henri, on the other hand, is eminently civilised and sane, and possesses a complete and organic theory on the ways to survive in Lager. He is only twenty-two, he is extremely intelligent, speaks French, German, English and Russian, has an excellent scientific and classical education.

His brother died in Buna last winter, and since then Henri has cut off every tie of affection; he has closed himself up, as if in armour, and fights to live without distraction with all the resources that he can derive from his quick intellect and his refined education. According to Henri's theory, there are three methods open to man to escape extermination which still allow him to retain the name of man: organisation, pity and theft.

He himself practises all three. There is no better strategist than Henri in seducing ('cultivating' he says) the English POWs. In his hands they become real geese with golden eggs – if you remember that in exchange for a single English cigarette you can make enough in the Lager not to starve for a day. Henri was once seen in the act of eating a real hard-boiled egg.

The traffic in products of English origin is Henri's monopoly, and this is all a matter of organisation; but his instrument of penetration, with the English and with others, is pity. Henri has the delicate and subtly perverse body and face of Sodoma's San Sebastian: his eyes are deep and profound, he has no beard yet, he moves with a natural languid elegance (although when necessary he knows how to run and jump like a cat, while the capacity of his stomach is little inferior to that of Elias). Henri is perfectly aware of his natural gifts and exploits them with the cold competence of a physicist using a scientific instrument: the results are surprising. Basically it is a question of a discovery: Henri has discovered that pity, being a primary and instinctive sentiment, grows quite well if ably cultivated, particularly in the primitive minds of the brutes who command us, those very brutes who have no scruples about beating us up without a reason, or treading our faces into the ground; nor has the great practical importance of the discovery escaped him, and upon it he has built up his personal trade.

As the ichneumon paralyses the great hairy caterpillar, wounding it in its only vulnerable ganglion, so Henri at a glance sizes up the subject, '*son type*'; he speaks to him briefly, to each with the appropriate language, and the '*type*' is conquered: he listens with increasing sympathy, he is moved by the fate of this unfortunate young man, and not much time is needed before he begins to yield returns.

There is no heart so hardened that Henri cannot breach it if he sets himself to it seriously. In the Lager, and in Buna as well, his protectors are very numerous: English soldiers, French, Ukrainian, Polish civilian workers: German 'politicals'; at least four *Blockältester*, a cook, even an SS man. But his favourite field is Ka-Be: Henri has free entry into Ka-Be; Doctor Citron and Doctor Weiss are more than his protectors, they are his friends and take him in whenever he wants and with the diagnosis he wants. This takes place especially immediately before selections, and in the periods of the most laborious work: 'hibernation', as he says.

Possessing such conspicuous friendships, it is natural that Henri is rarely reduced to the third method, theft; on the other hand, he naturally does not talk much about this subject.

It is very pleasant to talk to Henri in moments of rest. It is also useful: there is nothing in the camp that he does not know and about which he has not reasoned in his close and coherent manner. Of his conquests, he speaks with educated modesty, as of prey of little worth, but he digresses willingly into an explanation of the calculation which led him to approach Hans asking him about his son at the front, and Otto instead showing him the scars on his shins.

To speak with Henri is useful and pleasant: one sometimes also feels him warm and near; communication, even affection seems possible. One seems to glimpse, behind his uncommon personality, a human soul, sorrowful and aware of itself. But the next moment his sad smile freezes into a cold grimace which seems studied at the mirror; Henri politely excuses himself ('... *j'ai quelque chose à faire*', '... *j'ai quelqu'un à voir*') and here he is again, intent on his hunt and his struggle; hard and distant, enclosed in armour, the enemy of all, inhumanly cunning and incomprehensible like the Serpent in Genesis.

From all my talks with Henri, even the most cordial, I have always left with a slight taste of defeat; of also having been, somehow inadvertently, not a man to him, but an instrument in his hands.

I know that Henri is living today. I would give much to know his life as a free man, but I do not want to see him again.

10 Chemical Examination

Kommando 98, called the Chemical Kommando, should have been a squad of skilled workers.

The day on which its formation was officially announced a meagre group of fifteen Häftlinge gathered in the grey of dawn around the new Kapo in the roll-call square.

This was the first disillusion: he was a 'green triangle', a professional delinquent, the *Arbeitsdienst* had not thought it necessary for the Kapo of the Chemical Kommando to be a chemist. It was pointless wasting one's breath asking him questions; he would not have replied, or else he would have replied with kicks and shouts. On the other hand, his not very robust appearance and his smaller-than-average stature were reassuring.

He made a short speech in the foul German of the barracks, and the disillusion was confirmed. So these were the chemists: well, he was Alex, and if they thought they were entering paradise, they were mistaken. In the first place, until the day production began, Kommando 98 would be no more than an ordinary transport-Kommando attached to the magnesium chloride warehouse. Secondly, if they imagined, being *Intelligenten*, intellectuals, that they could make a fool of him, Alex, a *Reichsdeutscher*, well, *Herrgottsacrament*, he would show them, he would . . . (and with his fist clenched and index finger extended he cut across the air with the menacing gesture of the Germans); and finally, they should not imagine that they would fool anyone, if they had applied for the position without any qualification – an examination, yes gentlemen, in the very near future; a chemistry examination, before the triumvirate of the Polymerization Department: Doktor Hagen, Doktor Probst and Doktor Ingenieur Pannwitz.

And with this, *meine Herren*, enough time had been lost, Kommandos 96 and 97 had already started, forward march, and to begin with, whosoever failed to walk in line and step would have to deal with him.

He was a Kapo like all the other Kapos.

Leaving the camp, in front of the musical band and the SS counting-post we march in rows of five, beret in hand, arms hanging down our sides and neck rigid; speaking is forbidden. Then we change to threes and it is possible to exchange a few words amidst the clatter of ten thousand pairs of wooden shoes.

Who are my new comrades? Next to me walks Alberto; he is in his third year at university, and once again we have managed to stay together. The third person on my left I have never seen; he seems very young, is as pale as wax and has the number of the Dutch. The three backs in front of me are also new. It is dangerous to turn around, I might lose step or stumble; but I try for a moment, and see the face of Iss Clausner.

So long as one walks there is no time to think, one has to take care not to step on the shoes of the fellow hobbling in front, and not let them be stepped on by the fellow behind; every now and again there is a hole to be walked over, an oily puddle to be avoided. I know where we are, I have already come here with my preceding Kommando, it is the H-Strasse, the road of the stores, I tell Alberto, we are really going to the magnesium chloride warehouse, at least that was not a lie.

We have arrived, we climb down into a large damp cellar, full of draughts; this is the headquarters of the Kommando, the Bude as it is called here. The Kapo divides us into three squads: four to unload the sacks from the wagon, seven to carry them down, four to pile them up in the depot. We form the last squad, I, Alberto, Iss and the Dutchman.

At last we can speak, and to each one of us what Alex said seems a madman's dream.

With these empty faces of ours, with these sheared craniums, with these shameful clothes, to take a chemical examination. And obviously it will be in German; and we will have to go in front of some blond Aryan doctor hoping that we do not have to blow our noses, because perhaps he will not know that we do not have handkerchiefs, and it will certainly not be possible to explain it to him. And we will have our old comrade hunger with us, and we will hardly be able to stand still on our feet, and he will certainly smell our odour, to which we are by now accustomed, but which persecuted us during the first days, the odour of turnips and cabbages, raw, cooked and digested.

Exactly so, Clausner confirms. But have the Germans such great need of chemists? Or is it a new trick, a new machine '*pour faire chier les Juifs*'? Are they aware of the grotesque and absurd test asked of us, of us who are no longer alive, of us who have already gone half crazy in the dreary expectation of nothing?

Clausner shows me the bottom of his bowl. Where others have carved their numbers, and Alberto and I our names, Clausner has written: '*Ne pas chercher à comprendre.*'

Although we do not think for more than a few minutes a day, and then in a strangely detached and external manner, we well know that we will end in selections. I know that I am not made of the stuff of those who resist, I am too civilised, I still think too much, I use myself up at work. And now I also know that I can save myself if I become a Specialist, and that I will become a Specialist if I pass a chemistry examination.

131   Chemical Examination

Today, at this very moment as I sit writing at a table, I myself am not convinced that these things really happened.

Three days passed, three of those usual immemorable days, so long while they are passing, and so short afterwards, and we were already all tired of believing in the chemistry examination.

The Kommando was reduced to twelve men: three had disappeared in the customary manner of down there, perhaps into the hut next door, perhaps cancelled from this world. Of the twelve, five were not chemists; all five had immediately requested permission from Alex to return to their former Kommandos. They were given a few kicks, but unexpectedly, and by who knows whose authority, it was decided that they should remain as auxiliaries to the Chemical Kommando.

Down came Alex into the magnesium chloride yard and called us seven out to go and face the examination. We go like seven awkward chicks behind the hen, following Alex up the steps of the *Polimerisations-Büro*. We are in the lobby, there is a brass-plate on the door with the three famous names. Alex knocks respectfully, takes off his beret and enters. We can hear a quiet voice; Alex comes out again. '*Ruhe, jetzt. Warten,*' wait in silence.

We are satisfied with this. When one waits time moves smoothly without need to intervene and drive it forward, while when one works, every minute moves painfully and has to be laboriously driven away. We are always happy to wait; we are capable of waiting for hours with the complete obtuse inertia of spiders in old webs.

Alex is nervous, he walks up and down and we move out of his way each time. We too, each in our own way, are uneasy; only Mendi is not. Mendi is a rabbi; he comes from sub-Carpathian Russia, from that confusion of peoples where everyone speaks at least three languages, and Mendi speaks seven. He knows a great number of things; besides being a rabbi, he is a militant Zionist, a comparative philologist, he has been a partisan and a lawyer; he is not a chemist, but he wants to try all the same, he is a stubborn, courageous, keen little man.

Balla has a pencil and we all crowd around him. We are not sure if we still know how to write, we want to try.

Kohlenwasserstoffe, Massenwirkungsgesetz. The German names of compounds and laws float back into my memory. I feel grateful towards my brain: I have not paid much attention to it, but it still serves me so well.

Here is Alex. I am a chemist. What have I to do with this man Alex? He plants his feet in front of me, he roughly adjusts the collar of my jacket, he takes out my beret and slaps it on my head, then he steps backwards, eyes the result with a disgusted air, and turns his back, muttering: '*Was für ein Muselmann Zugang.*' What a messy recruit!

The door opens. The three doctors have decided that six candidates will be examined in the morning. The seventh will not. I am the seventh, I have the highest entry number, I have to return to work. Alex will only come to fetch me in the afternoon. What ill-luck, I cannot even talk to the others to hear what questions they are asking.

This time it really is my turn. Alex looks at me blackly on the doorstep; he feels himself in some way responsible for my miserable appearance. He dislikes me because I am Italian, because I am Jewish and because of all of us, I am the one furthest from his sergeants' mess ideal of virility. By analogy, without understanding anything, and proud of this very ignorance, he shows a profound disbelief in my chances for the examination.

We have entered. There is only Doktor Pannwitz; Alex, beret in hand, speaks to him in an undertone: '. . . an Italian, has been here

only three months, already half kaput . . . *Er sagt er ist Chemiker . . .'*
But he, Alex, apparently has his reservations on the subject.

Alex is briefly dismissed and put aside, and I feel like Oedipus in
front of the Sphinx. My ideas are clear, and I am aware even at this
moment that the position at stake is important; yet I feel a mad
desire to disappear, not to take the test.

Pannwitz is tall, thin, blond; he has eyes, hair and nose as all
Germans ought to have them, and sits formidably behind a complicated writing-table. I, Häftling 174517, stand in his office, which
is a real office, shining, clean and ordered, and I feel that I would
leave a dirty stain on whatever I touched.

When he finished writing, he raised his eyes and looked at me.

From that day I have thought about Doktor Pannwitz many
times and in many ways. I have asked myself how he really functioned as a man; how he filled his time, outside of the Polymerization and the Indo-Germanic conscience; above all when I was once
more a free man, I wanted to meet him again, not from a spirit of
revenge, but merely from a personal curiosity about the human
soul.

Because that look was not one between two men; and if I had
known how completely to explain the nature of that look, which
came as if across the glass window of an aquarium between two
beings who live in different worlds, I would also have explained the
essence of the great insanity of the third Germany.

One felt in that moment, in an immediate manner, what we all
thought and said of the Germans. The brain which governed those
blue eyes and those manicured hands said: 'This something in front
of me belongs to a species which it is obviously opportune to suppress. In this particular case, one has first to make sure that it does
not contain some utilisable element.' And in my head, like seeds in
an empty pumpkin: 'Blue eyes and fair hair are essentially wicked.

No communication possible. I am a specialist in mine chemistry. I am a specialist in organic syntheses. I am a specialist . . .'

And the interrogation began, while in the corner that third zoological specimen, Alex, yawned and chewed noisily.

'*Wo sind Sie geboren?*' He addresses me as *Sie*, the polite form of address: Doktor Ingenieur Pannwitz has no sense of humour. Curse him, he is not making the slightest effort to speak a slightly more comprehensible German.

I took my degree at Turin in 1941, *summa cum laude* – and while I say it I have the definite sensation of not being believed, of not even believing it myself; it is enough to look at my dirty hands covered with sores, my convict's trousers encrusted with mud. Yet I am he, the B.Sc. of Turin, in fact, at this particular moment it is impossible to doubt my identity with him, as my reservoir of knowledge of organic chemistry, even after so long an inertia, responds at request with unexpected docility. And even more, this sense of lucid elation, this excitement which I feel warm in my veins, I recognise it, it is the fever of examinations, *my* fever of *my* examinations, that spontaneous mobilisation of all my logical faculties and all my knowledge, which my friends at university so envied me.

The examination is going well. As I gradually realise it, I seem to grow in stature. He is asking me now on what subject I wrote my degree thesis. I have to make a violent effort to recall that sequence of memories, so deeply buried away: it is as if I was trying to remember the events of a previous incarnation.

Something protects me. My poor old 'Measurements of dielectrical constants' are of particular interest to this blond Aryan who lives so safely: he asks me if I know English, he shows me Gatterman's book, and even this is absurd and impossible, that down here, on the other side of the barbed wire, a Gatterman should exist, exactly similar to the one I studied in Italy in my fourth year, at home.

Now it is over: the excitement which sustained me for the whole of the test suddenly gives way and, dull and flat, I stare at the fair skin of his hand writing down my fate on the white page in incomprehensible symbols.

'*Los, ab!*' Alex enters the scene again, I am once more under his jurisdiction. He salutes Pannwitz, clicking his heels, and in return receives a faint nod of the eyelids. For a moment I grope around for a suitable formula of leave-taking: but in vain. I know how to say to eat, to work, to steal, to die in German; I also know how to say sulphuric acid, atmospheric pressure, and short-wave generator, but I do not know how to address a person of importance.

Here we are again on the steps. Alex flies down the stairs: he has leather shoes because he is not a Jew, he is as light on his feet as the devils of Malebolge. At the bottom he turns and looks at me sourly as I walk down hesitantly and noisily in my two enormous unpaired wooden shoes, clinging on to the rail like an old man.

It seems to have gone well, but I would be crazy to rely on it. I already know the Lager well enough to realise that one should never anticipate, especially optimistically. What is certain is that I have spent a day without working, so that tonight I will have a little less hunger, and this is a concrete advantage, not to be taken away.

To re-enter Bude, one has to cross a space cluttered up with piles of cross-beams and metal frames. The steel cable of a crane cuts across the road, and Alex catches hold of it to climb over: *Donnerwetter*, he looks at his hand black with thick grease. In the mean while I have joined him. Without hatred and without sneering, Alex wipes his hand on my shoulder, both the palm and the back of the hand, to clean it; he would be amazed, the poor brute Alex, if someone told him that today, on the basis of this action, I judge him and Pannwitz and the innumerable others like him, big and small, in Auschwitz and everywhere.

11 The Canto of Ulysses

There were six of us, scraping and cleaning the inside of an underground petrol tank; the daylight only reached us through a small manhole. It was a luxury job because no one supervised us; but it was cold and damp. The powder of the rust burnt under our eyelids and coated our throats and mouths with a taste almost like blood.

The rope-ladder hanging from the manhole began to sway: someone was coming. Deutsch extinguished his cigarette, Goldner woke Sivadjan; we all began to scrape the resonant steel-plate wall vigorously.

It was not the *Vorarbeiter*, it was only Jean, the *Pikolo* of our Kommando. Jean was an Alsatian student; although he was already twenty-four, he was the youngest Häftling of the Chemical Kommando. So that he was given the post of Pikolo, which meant the messenger-clerk, responsible for the cleaning of the hut, for the distribution of tools, for the washing of bowls and for keeping record of the working hours of the Kommando.

Jean spoke French and German fluently: as soon as we recognised his shoes on the top step of the ladder we all stopped scraping.

'*Also, Pikolo, was gibt es Neues?*'

'*Qu'est ce qu'il y a comme soupe aujourd' hui?*'

. . . in what mood was the Kapo? And the affair of the twenty-five lashes given to Stern? What was the weather like outside? Had he read the newspaper? What smell was coming from the civilian kitchen? What was the time?

Jean was liked a great deal by the Kommando. One must realise that the post of Pikolo represented a quite high rank in the hierarchy of the Prominents: the Pikolo (who is usually no more than seventeen years old) does no manual work, has an absolute right to the remainder of the daily ration to be found on the bottom of the vat and can stay all day near the stove. He 'therefore' has the right to a supplementary half-ration and has a good chance of becoming the friend and confidant of the Kapo, from whom he officially receives discarded clothes and shoes. Now Jean was an exceptional Pikolo. He was shrewd and physically robust, and at the same time gentle and friendly: although he continued his secret individual struggle against death, he did not neglect his human relationships with less privileged comrades; at the same time he had been so able and persevering that he had managed to establish himself in the confidence of Alex, the Kapo.

Alex had kept all his promises. He had shown himself a violent and unreliable rogue, with an armour of solid and compact ignorance and stupidity, always excepting his intuition and consummate technique as convict-keeper. He never let slip an opportunity to proclaim his pride in his pure blood and his green triangle, and displayed a lofty contempt for his ragged and starving chemists: '*Ihr Doktoren! Ihr Intelligenten!*' he sneered every day, watching them crowd around with their bowls held out for the distribution of the ration. He was extremely compliant and servile before the civilian Meister and with the SS he kept up ties of cordial friendship.

He was clearly intimidated by the register of the Kommando and by the daily report of work, and this had been the path that Pikolo had chosen to make himself indispensable. It had been a long, cautious and subtle task which the entire Kommando had followed for a month with bated breath; but at the end the porcupine's defence was penetrated, and Pikolo confirmed in his office to the satisfaction of all concerned.

Although Jean had never abused his position, we had already been able to verify that a single word of his, said in the right tone of voice and at the right moment, had great power; many times already it had saved one of us from a whipping or from being denounced to the SS. We had been friends for a week: we discovered each other during the unusual occasion of an air-raid alarm, but then, swept by the fierce rhythm of the Lager, we had only been able to greet each other fleetingly, at the latrines, in the washroom.

Hanging with one hand on the swaying ladder, he pointed to me: '*Aujourd'hui c'est Primo qui viendra avec moi chercher la soupe.*'

Until yesterday it had been Stern, the squinting Transylvanian; now he had fallen into disgrace for some story of brooms stolen from the store, and Pikolo had managed to support my candidature as assistant to the '*Essenholen*', the daily corvée of the ration.

He climbed out and I followed him, blinking in the brightness of the day. It was warmish outside, the sun drew a faint smell of paint and tar from the greasy earth, which made me think of a holiday beach of my infancy. Pikolo gave me one of the two wooden poles, and we walked along under a clear June sky.

I began to thank him, but he stopped me: it was not necessary. One could see the Carpathians covered in snow. I breathed in the fresh air, I felt unusually light-hearted.

'*Tu es fou de marcher si vite. On a le temps, tu sais.*' The ration was collected half a mile away; one had to return with the pot weighing over 100 pounds supported on the two poles. It was quite a tiring task, but it meant a pleasant walk there without a load, and the ever-welcome chance of going near the kitchens.

We slowed down. Pikolo was expert. He had chosen the path cleverly so that we would have to make a long detour, walking at least for an hour, without arousing suspicion. We spoke of our houses, of Strasbourg and Turin, of the books we had read, of what we had studied, of our mothers: how all mothers resemble each other! His mother too had scolded him for never knowing how much money he had in his pocket; his mother too would have been amazed if she had known that he had found his feet, that day by day he was finding his feet.

An SS man passed on a bicycle. It is Rudi, the *Blockführer*. Halt! Attention! Take off your beret! '*Sale brute, celui-là. Ein ganz gemeiner Hund.*' Can he speak French and German with equal facility? Yes, he thinks indifferently in both languages. He spent a month in Liguria, he likes Italy, he would like to learn Italian. I would be pleased to teach him Italian: why not try? We can do it. Why not immediately, one thing is as good as another, the important thing is not to lose time, not to waste this hour.

Limentani from Rome walks by, dragging his feet, with a bowl hidden under his jacket. Pikolo listens carefully, picks up a few words of our conversation and repeats them smiling: '*Zup-pa, campo, acqua.*'

Frenkl the spy passes. Quicken our pace, one never knows, he does evil for evil's sake.

. . . The canto of Ulysses. Who knows how or why it comes into my mind. But we have no time to change, this hour is already less than an hour. If Jean is intelligent he will understand. He *will* understand – today I feel capable of so much.

. . . Who is Dante? What is the Comedy? That curious sensation of novelty which one feels if one tries to explain briefly what is the Divine Comedy. How the Inferno is divided up, what are its punishments. Virgil is Reason, Beatrice is Theology.

Jean pays great attention, and I begin slowly and accurately:

Then of that age-old fire the loftier horn
Began to mutter and move, as a wavering flame
Wrestles against the wind and is over-worn;
And, like a speaking tongue vibrant to frame
Language, the tip of it flickering to and fro
Threw out a voice and answered: 'When I came . . .'

Here I stop and try to translate. Disastrous – poor Dante and poor French! All the same, the experience seems to promise well: Jean admires the bizarre simile of the tongue and suggests the appropriate word to translate 'age-old'.

And after ' "When I came?" ' Nothing. A hole in my memory. ' "Before Aeneas ever named it so." ' Another hole. A fragment floats into my mind, not relevant: ' ". . . nor piety To my old father, not the wedded love That should have comforted Penelope . . ." ', is it correct?

'. . . So on the open sea I set forth.'

Of this I am certain, I am sure, I can explain it to Pikolo, I can point out why ' "I set forth" '* is not 'je me mis', it is much stronger and more audacious, it is a chain which has been broken, it is throwing oneself on the other side of a barrier, we know the impulse well. The open sea: Pikolo has travelled by sea, and knows what it means: it is when the horizon closes in on itself, free, straight ahead and simple, and there is nothing but the smell of the sea; sweet things, ferociously far away.

We have arrived at Kraftwerk, where the cable-laying Kommando works. Engineer Levi must be here. Here he is, one can only see his head above the trench. He waves to me, he is a brave

* 'misi me' [translator's note].

man, I have never seen his morale low, he never speaks of eating.

‘ “Open sea” ’, ‘ “open sea” ’, I know it rhymes with ‘ “left me” ’:
‘ “. . . and that small band of comrades that had never left me” ’,
but I cannot remember if it comes before or after. And the journey
as well, the foolhardy journey beyond the Pillars of Hercules, how
sad, I have to tell it in prose – a sacrilege. I have only rescued two
lines, but they are worth stopping for:

‘. . . that none should prove so hardy
To venture the uncharted distance . . .’

‘ “to venture” ’*: I had to come to the Lager to realise that it is the
same expression as before: ‘ “I set forth” ’. But I say nothing to Jean,
I am not sure that it is an important observation. How many things
there are to say, and the sun is already high, midday is near. I am in
a hurry, a terrible hurry.

Here, listen Pikolo, open your ears and your mind, you have to
understand, for my sake:

‘ “Think of your breed; for brutish ignorance
Your mettle was not made; you were made men,
To follow after knowledge and excellence.” ’

As if I also was hearing it for the first time: like the blast of a
trumpet, like the voice of God. For a moment I forget who I am
and where I am.

Pikolo begs me to repeat it. How good Pikolo is, he is aware that
it is doing me good. Or perhaps it is something more: perhaps,
despite the wan translation and the pedestrian, rushed commentary, he has received the message, he has felt that it has to do with

* ‘*si metta*’ [translator’s note].

him, that it has to do with all men who toil, and with us in particular; and that it has to do with us two, who dare to reason of these things with the poles for the soup on our shoulders.

'My little speech made every one so keen . . .'

. . . and I try, but in vain, to explain how many things this ' "keen" ' means. There is another lacuna here, this time irreparable. ' ". . . the light kindles and grows Beneath the moon" ' or something like it; but before it? . . . Not an idea, 'keine Ahnung' as they say here. Forgive me, Pikolo, I have forgotten at least four triplets.
'Ça ne fait rien, vas-y tout de même.'

'. . . When at last hove up a mountain, grey
With distance, and so lofty and so steep,
I never had seen the like on any day.'

Yes, yes, ' "so lofty and so steep" ', not 'very steep',* a consecutive proposition. And the mountains when one sees them in the distance . . . the mountains . . . oh, Pikolo, Pikolo, say something, speak, do not let me think of my mountains which used to show up against the dusk of evening as I returned by train from Milan to Turin!

Enough, one must go on, these are things that one thinks but does not say. Pikolo waits and looks at me.

I would give today's soup to know how to connect ' "the like on any day" ' to the last lines. I try to reconstruct it through the rhymes, I close my eyes, I bite my fingers – but it is no use, the rest is silence. Other verses dance in my head: '. . . The sodden ground belched wind . . .', no, it is something else. It is late, it is late, we have reached the kitchen, I must finish:

* 'alta tanto', not 'molto alta' [translator's note].

'And three times round she went in roaring smother
With all the waters; at the fourth the poop
Rose, and the prow went down, as pleased Another.'

I keep Pikolo back, it is vitally necessary and urgent that he listen, that he understand this ' "as pleased Another" ' before it is too late; tomorrow he or I might be dead, or we might never see each other again, I must tell him, I must explain to him about the Middle Ages, about the so human and so necessary and yet unexpected anachronism, but still more, something gigantic that I myself have only just seen, in a flash of intuition, perhaps the reason for our fate, for our being here today . . .

We are now in the soup queue, among the sordid, ragged crowd of soup-carriers from other Kommandos. Those just arrived press against our backs. '*Kraut und Rüben? Kraut und Rüben.*' The official announcement is made that the soup today is cabbage and turnip: '*Choux et navets. Kaposzta és répak.*'

'And over our heads the hollow seas closed up.'

12 The Events of the Summer

Throughout the spring, convoys arrived from Hungary; one prisoner in two was Hungarian, and Hungarian had become the second language in the camp after Yiddish.

In the month of August 1944, we who had entered the camp five months before now counted among the old ones. As such, we of Kommando 98 were not amazed that the promises made to us and the examination we had passed had brought no result; neither amazed nor exceptionally saddened. At bottom, we all had a certain dread of changes: 'When things change, they change for the worse' was one of the proverbs of the camp. More generally, experience had shown us many times the vanity of every conjecture: why worry oneself trying to read into the future when no action, no word of ours could have the minimum influence? We were old Häftlinge: our wisdom lay in 'not trying to understand', not imagining the future, not tormenting ourselves as to how and when it would all be over; not asking others or ourselves any questions.

We preserved the memories of our previous life, but blurred and remote, profoundly sweet and sad, like the memories of early infancy. While for everybody, the moment of entry into the camp was the starting-point of a different sequence of thoughts, those near and sharp, continually confirmed by present experience, like wounds reopened every day.

The news heard in the Buna yards of the Allied landing in Normandy, of the Russian offensive and of the failed attempt against Hitler, had given rise to waves of violent but ephemeral hope. Day by day everyone felt his strength vanish, his desire to live melt away, his mind grow dim; and Normandy and Russia were so far away,

and the winter so near; hunger and desolation so concrete, and all the rest so unreal, that it did not seem possible that there could really exist any other world or time other than our world of mud and our sterile and stagnant time, whose end we were by now incapable of imagining.

For living men, the units of time always have a value, which increases in ratio to the strength of the internal resources of the person living through them; but for us, hours, days, months spilled out sluggishly from the future into the past, always too slowly, a valueless and superfluous material, of which we sought to rid ourselves as soon as possible. With the end of the season when the days chased each other, vivacious, precious and irrecoverable, the future stood in front of us, grey and inarticulate, like an invincible barrier. For us, history had stopped.

But in August '44 the bombardments of Upper Silesia began, and they continued with irregular pauses and renewals throughout the summer and the autumn until the definite crisis.

The monstrously unanimous labour of gestation of the Buna stopped brusquely, and at once degenerated into a disconnected, frantic and paroxysmal confusion. The day on which the production of synthetic rubber should have begun, which seemed imminent in August, was gradually postponed until the Germans no longer spoke about it.

Constructive work stopped; the power of the countless multitudes of slaves was directed elsewhere, and day by day showed itself more riotous and passively hostile. At every raid there was new damage to be repaired; the delicate machinery assembled with care just before had to be dismantled again and evacuated; air-raid shelters and walls had to be hurriedly erected to show themselves at the next test as ironically ineffective as sand-castles.

We had thought that anything would be preferable to the monotony of the identical and inexorably long days, to the systematic and ordered squalor of the Buna at work; but we were forced to change our minds when the Buna began to fall in pieces around us, as if struck by a curse in which we ourselves felt involved. We had to sweat amidst the dust and smoking ruins, and tremble like beasts, flattened against the earth by the anger of aeroplanes; broken by exhaustion and parched with thirst, we returned in the long, windy evenings of the Polish summer to find the camp upside-down, no water to drink or wash in, no soup for our empty bellies, no light by which to defend our piece of bread against someone else's hunger, or find our shoes and clothes in the morning in the dark, shrieking hole of the Block.

At Buna the German civilians raged with the fury of the secure man who wakes up from a long dream of domination and sees his own ruin and is unable to understand it. The *Reichsdeutsche* of the Lager as well, politicals included, felt the ties of blood and soil in the hour of danger. This new fact reduced the complications of hatreds and incomprehensions to their elementary terms and re-divided the camp: the politicals, together with the green triangles and the SS, saw, or thought they saw, in all our faces the mockery of revenge and the vicious joy of the vendetta. They found themselves in unanimous agreement on this, and their ferocity redoubled. No German could now forget that we were on the other side: on the side of the terrible sowers who furrowed the German sky as masters, high above every defence, and twisted the living metal of their constructions, carrying slaughter every day into their very homes, into the hitherto unviolated homes of the German people.

As for us, we were too destroyed to be really afraid. The few who could still judge and feel rightly, drew new strength and hope from the bombardments; those whom hunger had not yet reduced to a definitive inertia often profited from the moments of general panic to undertake doubly rash expeditions (since, besides the direct risk of the raid, theft carried out in conditions of emergency was punished by hanging) to the factory kitchens or the stores. But the greater number bore the new danger and the new discomforts with unchanged indifference: it was not a conscious resignation, but the opaque torpor of beasts broken-in by blows, whom the blows no longer hurt.

Entry to the reinforced shelters was forbidden us. When the earth began to tremble, we dragged ourselves, stunned and limping, through the corrosive fumes of the smoke bombs to the vast waste areas, sordid and sterile, closed within the boundary of the Buna; there we lay inert, piled up on top of each other like dead men, but still aware of the momentary pleasure of our bodies resting. We looked with indifferent eyes at the smoke and flames breaking out around us: in moments of quiet, full of the distant menacing roar that every European knows, we picked from the ground the stunted chicory leaves and dandelions, trampled on a hundred times, and chewed them slowly in silence.

When the alarm was over, we returned from all parts to our posts, a silent innumerable flock, accustomed to the anger of men and things; and continued that work of ours, as hated as ever, now even more obviously useless and senseless.

In this world shaken every day more deeply by the omens of its nearing end, amidst new terrors and hopes, with intervals of exasperated slavery, I happened to meet Lorenzo.

The story of my relationship with Lorenzo is both long and short, plain and enigmatic: it is the story of a time and condition now effaced from every present reality, and so I do not think it can be understood except in the manner in which we nowadays understand events of legends or the remotest history.

In concrete terms it amounts to little: an Italian civilian worker brought me a piece of bread and the remainder of his ration every day for six months; he gave me a vest of his, full of patches; he wrote a postcard on my behalf to Italy and brought me the reply. For all this he neither asked nor accepted any reward, because he was good and simple and did not think that one did good for a reward.

All this should not sound little. My case was not the only one; as has already been said, there were others of us who had contacts of various kinds with civilians, and derived from them the means to survive; but they were relationships of a different nature. Our comrades spoke of them in the same ambiguous manner, full of overtones, in which men of the world speak of their feminine relationships: that is, of adventures of which one can justly be proud and for which one wants to be envied, but which, even for the most pagan consciences, always remain on the margins of the permissible and the honest; so that it is incorrect and improper to boast about them. It is in this way that the Häftlinge speak of their civilian 'protectors' and 'friends'; with an ostentatious discretion, without stating names, so as not to compromise them, and especially and above all so as not to create undesirable rivals. The most consummate, the professional seducers like Henri, do not in fact speak of them; they surround their successes with an aura of equivocal mystery, and they limit themselves to hints and allusions, calculated to arouse in their audience a confused and disquieting legend that they enjoy the good graces of boundlessly powerful and generous civilians. This in view of a deliberate aim: the reputation of good luck, as we have said elsewhere, shows itself of fundamental utility to whosoever knows how to surround himself by it.

The reputation of being a seducer, of being 'organised', excites at once envy, scorn, contempt and admiration. Whoever allows himself to be seen eating 'organised' food is judged quite severely; he shows a serious lack of modesty and tact, besides an open stupidity. It would be equally stupid and impertinent to ask 'who gave it to you? where did you find it? how did you manage it?' Only the High Numbers, foolish, useless and helpless, who know nothing of the rules of the Lager, ask such questions; one does not reply to these questions, or one replies '*Verschwinde, Mensch!*', '*Hau' ab*', '*Uciekaj*', '*Schiess in den Wind*', '*Va chier*'; in short, with one of those countless equivalents of 'Go to hell' in which camp jargon is so rich.

There are also those who specialise in complex and patient spying campaigns to identify who is the civilian or group of civilians to whom so-and-so turns, and then try in various ways to supplant him. Interminable controversies of priority break out, made all the more bitter for the loser by the knowledge that a 'tried' civilian is almost more profitable, and above all safer than a civilian making his first contact with us. He is a civilian who is worth much more for obvious sentimental and technical reasons: he already knows the principles of the 'organisation', its regulations and dangers, and even more he has shown himself capable of overcoming the caste barrier.

In fact, we are the untouchables to the civilians. They think, more or less explicitly – with all the nuances lying between contempt and commiseration – that as we have been condemned to this life of ours, reduced to our condition, we must be tainted by some mysterious, grave sin. They hear us speak in many different languages, which they do not understand and which sound to them as grotesque as animal noises; they see us reduced to ignoble slavery, without hair, without honour and without names, beaten every day, more abject every day, and they never see in our eyes a light of rebellion, or of peace, or of faith. They know us as thieves and untrustworthy, muddy, ragged and starving, and mistaking the effect for the cause, they judge us worthy of our abasement. Who could tell one of our faces from the other? For them we are '*Kazett*', a singular neuter word.

This naturally does not stop many of them throwing us a piece of bread or a potato now and again, or giving us their bowls, after the distribution of the '*Zivilsuppe*' in the work-yards, to scrape and give back washed. They do it to get rid of some importunate starved look, or through a momentary impulse of humanity, or through simple curiosity to see us running from all sides to fight each other for the scrap, bestially and without restraint, until the strongest one gobbles it up, whereupon all the others limp away, frustrated.

Now nothing of this sort occurred between me and Lorenzo. However little sense there may be in trying to specify why I, rather than thousands of others, managed to survive the test, I believe that it was really due to Lorenzo that I am alive today; and not so much for his material aid, as for his having constantly reminded me by his presence, by his natural and plain manner of being good, that there still existed a just world outside our own, something and someone still pure and whole, not corrupt, not savage, extraneous to hatred and terror; something difficult to define, a remote possibility of good, but for which it was worth surviving.

The personages in these pages are not men. Their humanity is buried, or they themselves have buried it, under an offence received or inflicted on someone else. The evil and insane SS men, the Kapos, the politicals, the criminals, the Prominents, great and small, down to the indifferent slave Häftlinge, all the grades of the mad hierarchy created by the Germans paradoxically fraternised in a uniform internal desolation.

But Lorenzo was a man; his humanity was pure and uncontaminated, he was outside this world of negation. Thanks to Lorenzo, I managed not to forget that I myself was a man.

13 October 1944

We fought with all our strength to prevent the arrival of winter. We clung to all the warm hours, at every dusk we tried to keep the sun in the sky for a little longer, but it was all in vain. Yesterday evening the sun went down irrevocably behind a confusion of dirty clouds, chimney-stacks and wires, and today it is winter.

We know what it means because we were here last winter; and the others will soon learn. It means that in the course of these months, from October till April, seven out of ten of us will die. Whoever does not die will suffer minute by minute, all day, every day: from the morning before dawn until the distribution of the evening soup we will have to keep our muscles continually tensed, dance from foot to foot, beat our arms under our shoulders against the cold. We will have to spend bread to acquire gloves, and lose hours of sleep to repair them when they become unstitched. As it will no longer be possible to eat in the open, we will have to eat our meals in the hut, on our feet, everyone will be assigned an area of floor as large as a hand, as it is forbidden to rest against the bunks. Wounds will open on everyone's hands, and to be given a bandage will mean waiting every evening for hours on one's feet in the snow and wind.

Just as our hunger is not that feeling of missing a meal, so our way of being cold has need of a new word. We say 'hunger', we say 'tiredness', 'fear', 'pain', we say 'winter' and they are different things. They are free words, created and used by free men who lived in comfort and suffering in their homes. If the Lagers had lasted longer a new, harsh language would have been born; and only this language could express what it means to toil the whole day in the wind, with the temperature below freezing, wearing only a shirt, underpants, cloth jacket and trousers, and in one's body nothing but weakness, hunger and knowledge of the end drawing nearer.

In the same way in which one sees a hope end, winter arrived this morning. We realised it when we left the hut to go and wash: there were no stars, the dark cold air had the smell of snow. In the roll-call square, in the grey of dawn, when we assembled for work, no one spoke. When we saw the first flakes of snow, we thought that if at the same time last year they had told us that we would have seen another winter in Lager, we would have gone and touched the electric wire-fence; and that even now we would go if we were logical, were it not for this last senseless crazy residue of unavoidable hope.

Because 'winter' means yet another thing.

Last spring the Germans had constructed huge tents in an open space in the Lager. For the whole of the good season each of them had catered for over a thousand men: now the tents had been taken down, and an excess two thousand guests crowded our huts. We old prisoners knew that the Germans did not like these irregularities and that something would soon happen to reduce our number.

One feels the selections arriving. '*Selekcja*': the hybrid Latin-and-Polish word is heard once, twice, many times, interpolated in foreign conversations; at first we cannot distinguish it, then it forces itself on our attention, and in the end it persecutes us.

This morning the Poles had said '*Selekcja*'. The Poles are the first to find out the news, and they generally try not to let it spread around, because to know something which the others still do not know can always be useful. By the time that everyone realises that a selection is imminent, the few possibilities of evading it (corrupting some doctor or some Prominent with bread or tobacco; leaving the hut for Ka-Be or vice versa at the right moment so as to cross with the commission) are already their monopoly.

In the days which follow, the atmosphere of the Lager and the yard is filled with '*Selekcja*': nobody knows anything definite, but all speak about it, even the Polish, Italian, French civilian workers whom we secretly see in the yard. Yet the result is hardly a wave of despondency: our collective morale is too inarticulate and flat to be unstable. The fight against hunger, cold and work leaves little margin for thought, even for this thought. Everybody reacts in his own way, but hardly anyone with those attitudes which would seem the most plausible as the most realistic, that is, with resignation or despair.

All those able to find a way out, try to take it; but they are the minority because it is very difficult to escape from a selection. The Germans apply themselves to these things with great skill and diligence.

Whoever is unable to prepare for it materially, seeks defence elsewhere. In the latrines, in the washroom, we show each other our chests, our buttocks, our thighs, and our comrades reassure us: 'You are all right, it will certainly not be your turn this time . . . *du bist kein Muselmann* . . . more probably mine . . .' and they undo their braces in turn and pull up their shirts.

Nobody refuses this charity to another: nobody is so sure of his own lot to be able to condemn others. I brazenly lied to old Wertheimer; I told him that if they questioned him, he should reply that he was forty-five, and he should not forget to have a shave the evening before, even if it cost him a quarter-ration of bread; apart from that he need have no fears, and in any case it was by no means certain that it was a selection for the gas chamber; had he not heard the *Blockältester* say that those chosen would go to Jaworszno to a convalescent camp?

It is absurd of Wertheimer to hope: he looks sixty, he has

enormous varicose veins, he hardly even notices the hunger any more. But he lies down on his bed, serene and quiet, and replies to someone who asks him with my own words; they are the command-words in the camp these days: I myself repeated them just as – apart from details – Chajim told them to me, Chajim, who has been in Lager for three years, and being strong and robust is wonderfully sure of himself; and I believed them.

On this slender basis I also lived through the great selection of October 1944 with inconceivable tranquillity. I was tranquil because I managed to lie to myself sufficiently. The fact that I was not selected depended above all on chance and does not prove that my faith was well founded.

Monsieur Pinkert is also, a priori, condemned: it is enough to look at his eyes. He calls me over with a sign, and with a confidential air tells me that he has been informed – he cannot tell me the source of information – that this time there is really something new: the Holy See, by means of the International Red Cross . . . in short, he personally guarantees both for himself and for me, in the most absolute manner, that every danger is ruled out; as a civilian he was, as is well known, attaché to the Belgian embassy at Warsaw.

Thus in various ways, even those days of vigil, which in the telling seem as if they ought to have passed every limit of human torment, went by not very differently from other days.

The discipline in both the Lager and Buna is in no way relaxed: the work, cold and hunger are sufficient to fill up every thinking moment.

Today is working Sunday, *Arbeitssonntag*: we work until 1 p.m., then we return to camp for the shower, shave and general control for skin diseases and lice. And in the yards, everyone knew mysteriously that the selection would be today.

The news arrived, as always, surrounded by a halo of contradictory or suspect details: the selection in the infirmary took place this morning; the percentage was seven per cent of the whole camp, thirty, fifty per cent of the patients. At Birkenau, the crematorium chimney has been smoking for ten days. Room has to be made for an enormous convoy arriving from the Poznan ghetto. The young tell the young that all the old ones will be chosen. The healthy tell the healthy that only the ill will be chosen. Specialists will be excluded. German Jews will be excluded. Low Numbers will be excluded. You will be chosen. I will be excluded.

At 1 p.m. exactly the yard empties in orderly fashion, and for two hours the grey unending army files past the two control stations where, as on every day, we are counted and recounted, and past the military band which for two hours without interruption plays, as on every day, those marches to which we must synchronise our steps at our entrance and our exit.

It seems like every day, the kitchen chimney smokes as usual, the distribution of the soup is already beginning. But then the bell is heard, and at that moment we realise that we have arrived.

Because this bell always sounds at dawn, when it means the reveille; but if it sounds during the day, it means 'Blocksperre', enclosure in huts, and this happens when there is a selection, to prevent anyone avoiding it, or when those selected leave for the gas, to prevent anyone seeing them leave.

Our Blockältester knows his business. He has made sure that we have all entered, he has the door locked, he has given everyone his card with his number, name, profession, age and nationality and he has ordered everyone to undress completely, except for shoes. We wait like this, naked, with the card in our hands, for the commission to reach our hut. We are hut 48, but one can never tell if they are going to begin at hut 1 or hut 60. At any rate, we can rest quietly at least for an hour, and there is no reason why we should not get under the blankets on the bunk and keep warm.

Many are already drowsing when a barrage of orders, oaths and blows proclaims the imminent arrival of the commission. The *Blockältester* and his helpers, starting at the end of the dormitory, drive the crowd of frightened, naked people in front of them and cram them in the *Tagesraum* which is the Quartermaster's office. The *Tagesraum* is a room seven yards by four: when the drive is over, a warm and compact human mass is jammed into the *Tagesraum*, perfectly filling all the corners, exercising such a pressure on the wooden walls as to make them creak.

Now we are all in the *Tagesraum*, and besides there being no time, there is not even any room in which to be afraid. The feeling of the warm flesh pressing all around is unusual and not unpleasant. One has to take care to hold up one's nose so as to breathe, and not to crumple or lose the card in one's hand.

The *Blockältester* has closed the connecting door and has opened the other two which lead from the dormitory and the *Tagesraum* outside. Here, in front of the two doors, stands the arbiter of our fate, an SS subaltern. On his right is the *Blockältester*, on his left, the Quartermaster of the hut. Each one of us, as he comes naked out of the *Tagesraum* into the cold October air, has to run the few steps between the two doors, give the card to the SS man and enter the dormitory door. The SS man, in the fraction of a second between two successive crossings, with a glance at one's back and front, judges everyone's fate, and in turn gives the card to the man on his right or his left, and this is the life or death of each of us. In three or four minutes a hut of two hundred men is 'done', as is the whole camp of twelve thousand men in the course of the afternoon.

Jammed in the charnel-house of the *Tagesraum*, I gradually felt the human pressure around me slacken, and in a short time it was my turn. Like everyone, I passed by with a brisk and elastic step, trying to hold my head high, my chest forward and my muscles contracted and conspicuous. With the corner of my eye I tried to look behind my shoulders, and my card seemed to end on the right.

As we gradually come back into the dormitory we are allowed to dress ourselves. Nobody yet knows with certainty his own fate, it has first of all to be established whether the condemned cards were those on the right or the left. By now there is no longer any point in sparing each other's feelings with superstitious scruples. Everybody crowds around the oldest, the most wasted-away, and most '*Muselmann*'; if their cards went to the left, the left is certainly the side of the condemned.

Even before the selection is over, everybody knows that the left was effectively the '*schlechte Seite*', the bad side. There have naturally been some irregularities: René, for example, so young and robust, ended on the left; perhaps it was because he has glasses, perhaps because he walks a little stooped like a myope, but more probably because of a simple mistake: René passed the commission immediately in front of me and there could have been a mistake with our cards. I think about it, discuss it with Alberto, and we agree that the hypothesis is probable; I do not know what I will think tomorrow and later; today I feel no distinct emotion.

It must equally have been a mistake about Sattler, a huge Transylvanian peasant who was still at home only twenty days ago; Sattler does not understand German, he has understood nothing of what has taken place, and stands in a corner mending his shirt. Must I go and tell him that his shirt will be of no more use?

There is nothing surprising about these mistakes: the examination is too quick and summary, and in any case, the important thing for the Lager is not that the most useless prisoners be eliminated, but that free posts be quickly created, according to a certain percentage previously fixed.

The selection is now over in our hut, but it continues in the others, so that we are still locked in. But as the soup-pots have arrived in the mean time, the *Blockältester* decides to proceed with the distribution at once. A double ration will be given to those selected. I have never discovered if this was a ridiculously charitable initiative of the *Blockältester*, or an explicit disposition of the SS, but in fact, in the interval of two or three days (sometimes even much longer) between the selection and the departure, the victims at Monowitz-Auschwitz enjoyed this privilege.

Ziegler holds out his bowl, collects his normal ration and then waits there expectantly. 'What do you want?' asks the *Blockältester*: according to him, Ziegler is entitled to no supplement, and he drives him away, but Ziegler returns and humbly persists. He was on the left, everybody saw it, let the *Blockältester* check the cards; he has the right to a double ration. When he is given it, he goes quietly to his bunk to eat.

Now everyone is busy scraping the bottom of his bowl with his spoon so as not to waste the last drops of the soup; a confused, metallic clatter, signifying the end of the day. Silence slowly prevails and then, from my bunk on the top row, I see and hear old Kuhn praying aloud, with his beret on his head, swaying backwards and forwards violently. Kuhn is thanking God because he has not been chosen.

Kuhn is out of his senses. Does he not see Beppo the Greek in the bunk next to him, Beppo who is twenty years old and is going to the gas chamber the day after tomorrow and knows it and lies there looking fixedly at the light without saying anything and without even thinking any more? Can Kuhn fail to realise that next time it will be his turn? Does Kuhn not understand that what has happened today is an abomination, which no propitiatory prayer, no pardon, no expiation by the guilty, which nothing at all in the power of man can ever clean again?

If I was God, I would spit at Kuhn's prayer.

14 Kraus

When it rains we would like to cry. It is November, it has been raining for ten days now and the ground is like the bottom of a swamp. Everything made of wood gives out a smell of mushrooms.

If I could walk ten steps to the left I would be under shelter in the shed; a sack to cover my shoulders would be sufficient, or even the prospect of a fire where I could dry myself; or even a dry rag to put between my shirt and my back. Between one movement of the shovel and another I think about it, and I really believe that to have a dry rag would be positive happiness.

By now it would be impossible to be wetter; I will just have to pay attention to move as little as possible, and above all not to make new movements, to prevent some other part of my skin coming into unnecessary contact with my soaking, icy clothes.

It is lucky that it is not windy today. Strange, how in some way one always has the impression of being fortunate, how some chance happening, perhaps infinitesimal, stops us crossing the threshold of despair and allows us to live. It is raining, but it is not windy. Or else, it is raining and is also windy: but you know that this evening it is your turn for the supplement of soup, so that even today you find the strength to reach the evening. Or it is raining, windy and you have the usual hunger, and then you think that if you really had to, if you really felt nothing in your heart but suffering and tedium – as sometimes happens, when you really seem to lie on the bottom – well, even in that case, at any moment you want you could always go and touch the electric wire-fence, or throw yourself under the shunting trains, and then it would stop raining.

*

161 Kraus

We have been stuck in the mud since the morning, legs akimbo, with our feet sinking ever deeper in the selfsame holes in the glutinous soil. We sway on our haunches at every swing of the shovel. I am half-way down the pit, Kraus and Clausner are at the bottom, Gounan is above me at surface level. Only Gounan can look around, and every now and again he warns Kraus curtly of the need to quicken the pace or even to rest, according to who is passing by in the road. Clausner uses the pickaxe, Kraus lifts the earth up to me on his shovel, and I gradually pass it up to Gounan who piles it up on one side. Others form a shuttle service with wheelbarrows and carry the earth somewhere, of no interest to us. Our world today is this hole of mud.

Kraus misses his stroke, a lump of mud flies up and splatters over my knees. It is not the first time it has happened, I warn him to be careful, but without much hope: he is Hungarian, he understands German badly and does not know a word of French. He is tall and thin, wears glasses and has a curious, small, twisted face; when he laughs he looks like a child, and he often laughs. He works too much and too vigorously: he has not yet learnt our underground art of economising on everything, on breath, movements, even thoughts. He does not yet know that it is better to be beaten, because one does not normally die of blows, but one does of exhaustion, and badly, and when one grows aware of it, it is already too late. He still thinks . . . oh no, poor Kraus, his is not reasoning, it is only the stupid honesty of a small employee, he brought it along with him, and he seems to think that his present situation is like outside, where it is honest and logical to work, as well as being of advantage, because according to what everyone says, the more one works the more one earns and eats.

'*Regardez-moi ça! . . . Pas si vite, idiot!*' Gounan swears at him from above; then he remembers to translate it in German:

'*Langsam, du blöder Einer, langsam, verstanden?*' Kraus can kill himself through exhaustion if he wants to, but not today, because we are working in a chain and the rhythm of the work is set by him.

There goes the siren of the Carbide factory, now the English prisoners are leaving; it is half-past four. Then the Ukrainian girls will leave and it will be five o'clock and we will be able to straighten our backs, and only the return march, the roll-call and the lice-control will separate us from our rest.

It is assembly time, '*Antreten*' from all sides; from all sides the mud puppets creep out, stretch their cramped limbs, carry the tools back to the huts. We extract our feet from the ditch cautiously so as not to let our shoes be sucked off, and leave, dripping and swaying, to line up for the return march. '*Zu dreine*', in threes. I tried to place myself near to Alberto as we had worked separately today and we both wanted to ask each other how it had gone; but someone hit me in the stomach and I finished behind him, right next to Kraus.

Now we leave. The Kapo marks time in a hard voice: '*Links, links, links*'; at first, our feet hurt, then we slowly grow warm and our nerves relax. We have bored our way through all the minutes of the day, this very day which seemed invincible and eternal this morning; now it lies dead and is immediately forgotten; already it is no longer a day, it has left no trace in anybody's memory. We know that tomorrow will be like today: perhaps it will rain a little more or a little less, or perhaps instead of digging soil we will go and unload bricks at the Carbide factory. Or the war might even finish tomorrow, or we might all be killed or transferred to another camp, or one of those great changes might take place which, ever since the Lager has been the Lager, have been indefatigably fore-told as imminent and certain. But who can seriously think about tomorrow?

163   Kraus

Memory is a curious instrument: ever since I have been in the camp, two lines written by a friend of mine a long time ago have been running through my mind:

> . . . Until one day
> there will be no more sense in saying: tomorrow.

It is like that here. Do you know how one says 'never' in camp slang? '*Morgen früh*', tomorrow morning.

It is now the hour of '*links, links, links und links*', the hour in which one must not lose step. Kraus is clumsy, he has already been kicked by the Kapo because he is incapable of walking in line: and now he is beginning to gesticulate and chew a miserable German, listen, listen, he wants to apologise for the spadeful of mud, he has not yet understood where we are, I must say Hungarians are really a most singular people.

To keep step and carry on a complicated conversation in German is too much. This time it is I who warn him that he has lost step; I look at him and I see his eyes behind the drops of water on his glasses, and they are the eyes of the man Kraus.

Then an important thing happened, and it is worth telling now, perhaps for the same reason that it happened then. I began to make a long speech to Kraus: in bad German, but slowly, separating the words, making sure after each sentence that he had understood.

I told him that I had dreamt that I was at home, the home where I was born, with my family, sitting with my legs under the table, and on the table a great deal, a very great deal to eat. And it was summer and it was in Italy – at Naples? . . . yes, at Naples, this is hardly the time to quibble. Then all of a sudden the bell rang, and I got up hurriedly and went to open the door, and who did I see? I saw him, this very Kraus Páli, with hair grown, clean and well nourished and dressed as a free man, with a loaf of bread in his hand. Yes, a loaf of four pounds, still warm. Then 'Servus, Páli, wie geht's?' and I felt filled with joy and made him come in, and I explained to my parents who he was, and that he had come from Budapest, and why he was so wet; because he was soaking, just like now. And I gave him food and drink and a good bed to sleep in, and it was night-time, but there was a wonderful warmth so that we were all dry in a moment (yes, I was also very wet).

What a good boy Kraus must have been as a civilian: he will not survive very long here, one can see it at the first glance, it is as logical as a theorem. I am sorry I do not know Hungarian, for his emotion has broken the dykes, and he is breaking out in a flood of outlandish Magyar words. I cannot understand anything except my name, but by the solemn gestures one would say that he is making promises and prophecies.

Poor silly Kraus. If he only knew that it is not true, that I have really dreamt nothing about him, that he is nothing to me except for a brief moment, nothing like everything is nothing down here, except the hunger inside and the cold and the rain around.

15 Die drei Leute vom Labor

How many months have gone by since we entered the camp? How many since the day I was dismissed from Ka-Be? And since the day of the chemistry examination? And since the October selection?

Alberto and I often ask ourselves these questions, and many others as well. There were ninety-six of us when we arrived, we, the Italians of convoy 174,000; only twenty-nine of us survived until October, and of these, eight went in the selection. We are now twenty-one and the winter has hardly begun. How many of us will be alive at the new year? How many when spring begins?

There have been no air raids now for several weeks; the November rain has turned to snow, and the snow has covered the ruins. The Germans and Poles go to work in rubber jackboots, woollen ear-pads and padded overalls; the English prisoners have their wonderful fur-lined jackets. They have distributed no overcoats in our Lager except to a few of the privileged; we are a specialised Kommando, which – in theory – only works under shelter; so we are left in our summer outfits.

We are the chemists, 'therefore' we work at the phenylbeta sacks. We cleared out the warehouse after the first air raids in the height of the summer. The phenylbeta seeped under our clothes and stuck to our sweating limbs and chafed us like leprosy; the skin came off our faces in large burnt patches. Then the air raids temporarily stopped and we carried the sacks back into the warehouse. Then the warehouse was hit and we took the sacks into the cellar of the Styrene Department. Now the warehouse has been repaired and once again we have to pile up the sacks there. The caustic smell of the phenylbeta impregnates our only suit, and follows us day and night like our shadows. So far, the advantages of being in the Chemical Kommando have been limited to the following: the others have received overcoats while we have not; the others carry 100-pound cement sacks, while we carry 125-pound phenylbeta sacks. How can we still think about the chemistry examination and our illusions of that time? At least four times during the summer we have heard speak of Doktor Pannwitz's laboratory in Bau 939, and the rumour spread that the analysts for the Polymerization Department would be chosen among us.

But now it is time to stop, it is all over now. This is the last act: the winter has begun, and with it our last battle. There is no longer any reason to doubt that it will be the last. Any time during the day when we happen to listen to the voice of our bodies, or ask our limbs, the answer is always the same: our strength will not last out. Everything around us speaks of a final decay and ruin. Half of Bau 939 is a heap of twisted metal and smashed concrete; large deformed blue icicles hang like pillars from the enormous tubings where the overheated steam used to roar. The Buna is silent now, and when the wind is propitious, if one listens hard, one can hear the continuous dull underground rumbling of the front which is getting nearer. Three hundred prisoners have arrived in the Lager from the Łódź ghetto, transferred by the Germans before the Russian advance: they told us rumours about the legendary battle of the Warsaw ghetto, and they described how the Germans had liquidated the Lublin camp over a year ago: four machine-guns in the corners and the huts set on fire; the civilised world will never know about it. When will it be our turn?

This morning the Kapo divided up the squads as usual. The Magnesium Chloride ten to the magnesium chloride: and they leave, dragging their feet, as slowly as possible, because the magnesium chloride is an extremely unpleasant job; you stand all day up to your ankles in cold, briny water, which soaks into your shoes, your clothes and your skin. The Kapo grabs hold of a brick and throws it among the group; they get clumsily out of the way, but do not quicken their pace. This is almost a custom, it happens every morning, and does not always mean that the Kapo has a definite intent to hurt.

The four of the *Scheisshaus*, to their work: and the four attached to the building of the new latrine leave. For when we exceeded the force of fifty Häftlinge with the arrival of the convoys from Łódź and Transylvania, the mysterious German bureaucrat who supervises these matters authorised us to build a '*Zweiplatziges Kommandoscheisshaus*', i.e. a two-seated closet reserved for our Kommando. We are not unaware of this mark of distinction, which makes ours one of the few Kommandos of which one can with reason boast one's membership: but it is evident that we will lose one of the simplest of pretexts to absent ourselves from work and arrange combinations with civilians. '*Noblesse oblige*,' says Henri, who has other strings to his bow.

The twelve for the bricks. Meister Dahm's five. The two for the tanks. How many absent? Three absent. Homolka gone into Ka-Be this morning, the ironsmith dead yesterday, François transferred who knows where or why. The roll-call is correct; the Kapo notes it down and is satisfied. There are only us eighteen of the phenylbeta left, beside the Prominents of the Kommando. And now the unexpected happens.

The Kapo says: Doktor Pannwitz has communicated to the *Arbeitsdienst* that three Häftlinge have been chosen for the Laboratory: 169509, Brackier; 175633, Kandel; 174517, Levi. For a moment my ears ring and the Buna whirls around me. There are three Levis in Kommando 98, but *Hundert Vierundsiebzig Fünf Hundert*

Siebzehn is me, there is no possible doubt. I am one of the three chosen.

The Kapo looks us up and down with a twisted smile. A Belgian, a Russian and an Italian: three '*Franzosen*', in short. Is it possible that three *Franzosen* have really been chosen to enter the paradise of the Laboratory?

Many comrades congratulate us; Alberto first of all, with genuine joy, without a shadow of envy. Alberto holds nothing against my fortune, he is really very pleased, both because of our friendship and because he will also gain from it. In fact, by now we two are bound by a tight bond of alliance, by which every 'organised' scrap is divided into two strictly equal parts. He has no reason to envy me, as he neither hoped nor desired to enter the Laboratory. The blood in his veins is too free for this untamed friend of mine to think of relaxing in a system; his instinct leads him elsewhere, to other solutions, towards the unforeseen, the impromptu, the new. Without hesitating, Alberto prefers the uncertainties and battles of the 'free profession' to a good employment.

I have a ticket from the *Arbeitsdienst* in my pocket, on which it is written that Häftling 174517, as a specialised worker, has the right to a new shirt and underpants and must be shaved every Wednesday.

The ravaged Buna lies under the first snows, silent and stiff like an enormous corpse; every day the sirens of the *Fliegeralarm* wail; the Russians are fifty miles away. The electric power station has stopped, the methanol rectification columns no longer exist, three of the four acetylene gasometers have been blown up. Prisoners 'reclaimed' from all the camps in east Poland pour into our Lager haphazardly; the minority are set to work, the majority leave immediately for Birkenau and the Chimney. The ration has been still further reduced. The Ka-Be is overflowing, the E-Häftlinge

have brought scarlet fever, diphtheria and petechial typhus into the camp.

But Häftling 174517 has been promoted as a Specialist and has the right to a new shirt and underpants and has to be shaved every Wednesday. No one can boast of understanding the Germans.

We entered the Laboratory timid, suspicious and bewildered like three wild beasts slinking into a large city. How clean and polished the floor is! It is a laboratory surprisingly like any other laboratory. Three long work-benches covered with hundreds of familiar objects. The glass instruments in a corner to drip, the precision balance, a Heraeus oven, a Höppler thermostat. The smell makes me start back as if from the blow of a whip: the weak aromatic smell of organic chemistry laboratories. For a moment the large semi-dark room at the university, my fourth year, the mild air of May in Italy come back to me with brutal violence and immediately vanish.

Herr Stawinoga gives us our workplaces. Stawinoga is a German Pole, still young, with an energetic, but sad and tired face. He is also Doktor: not of chemistry, but (*ne pas chercher à comprendre*) of comparative philology; all the same, he is head of the Laboratory. He does not speak to us willingly, but does not seem ill disposed. He calls us 'Monsieur' which is ridiculous and disconcerting.

The temperature in the Laboratory is wonderful; the thermometer reads 65 °F. We agree that they can make us wash the glass instruments, sweep the floor, carry the hydrogen flasks, anything so as to remain here, and so solve the problem of the winter for us. And then, on a second examination, even the problem of hunger should not be difficult to solve. Will they really want to search us at the exit every day? And even if they want to, will they do it every time that we ask to go to the latrine? Obviously not. And there is soap, petrol, alcohol here. I will stitch a secret pocket inside my jacket, and combine with the Englishman who works in the repairs yard and trades in petrol. We will see how strict the supervision is: but by now I have spent a year in the Lager and I know that if one wants to steal and seriously sets one's mind to it, no supervision and no searchings can prevent it.

So it would seem that fate, by a new unsuspected path, has arranged that we three, the object of envy of all the ten thousand condemned, suffer neither hunger nor cold this winter. This means a strong probability of not falling seriously ill, of not being frozen, of overcoming the selections. In these conditions, those less expert than us about things in the Lager might even be tempted by the hope of survival and by the thought of liberty. But we are not, we know how these matters go; all this is the gift of fortune, to be enjoyed as intensely as possible and at once; for there is no certainty about tomorrow. At the first glass I break, the first error in measurement, the first time my attention is distracted, I will go back to waste away in the snow and the winds until I am ready for the Chimney. And besides, who knows what will happen when the Russians come?

Because the Russians will come. The ground trembles day and night under our feet; the muffled dull rumbling of their artillery now bursts uninterrupted into the novel silence of the Buna. One breathes a tense air, an air of resolution. The Poles no longer work, the French again walk with their head high. The English wink at us and greet us aside with a V sign; and not always aside.

But the Germans are deaf and blind, enclosed in an armour of obstinacy and of wilful ignorance. Once again they have named the date for the beginning of the production of synthetic rubber: it will be the first of February 1945. They construct shelters and trenches, they repair the damage, they build, they fight, they command, they organise and they kill. What else could they do? They are Germans. This way of behaviour is not meditated and deliberate, but follows from their nature and from the destiny they have chosen. They could not act differently: if you wound the body of a dying man, the wound will begin to heal, even if the whole body dies within a day.

Every morning now, when the squads are divided, the Kapo calls us three of the Laboratory before all the others, '*die drei Leute vom Labor*'. In camp, in the evenings and the mornings, nothing distinguishes me from the flock, but during the day, at work, I am under shelter and warm, and nobody beats me; I steal and sell soap and petrol without risk, and perhaps I will be given a coupon for a pair of leather shoes. Even more, can this be called work? To work is to push wagons, carry sleepers, break stones, dig earth, press one's bare hands against the iciness of the freezing iron. But I sit all day, I have a notebook and a pencil and they have even given me a book to refresh my memory about analytical methods. I have a drawer where I can put my beret and gloves, and when I want to go out I only have to tell Herr Stawinoga, who never says no and asks no questions if I delay; he has the air of suffering in his flesh for the ruin which surrounds him.

My comrades in the Kommando envy me, and they are right; should I not be contented? But in the morning, I hardly escape the raging wind and cross the doorstep of the Laboratory when I find at my side the comrade of all my peaceful moments, of Ka-Be, of the rest-Sundays – the pain of remembering, the old ferocious suffering of feeling myself a man again, which attacks me like a dog the moment my conscience comes out of the gloom. Then I take my pencil and notebook and write what I would never dare tell anyone.

Then there are the women. How long is it since I have seen a woman? In Buna we quite often met the Polish and Ukrainian women workers, in trousers and leather jackets, huge and violent like their men. They were sweaty and dishevelled in the summer, padded out with thick clothes in the winter and worked with spades and pickaxes. We did not feel ourselves next to women.

It is different here. Faced with the girls of the Laboratory, we three feel ourselves sink into the ground from shame and embarrassment. We know what we look like: we see each other and sometimes we happen to see our reflection in a clean window. We are ridiculous and repugnant. Our cranium is bald on Monday, and covered by a short brownish mould by Saturday. We have a swollen and yellow face, marked permanently by the cuts made by the hasty barber, and often by bruises and numbed sores; our neck is long and knobbly, like that of plucked chickens. Our clothes are incredibly dirty, stained by mud, grease and blood; Kandel's breeches only arrive half-way down his calves, showing his bony, hairy ankles; my jacket runs off my shoulders as if off a wooden clothes-hanger. We are full of fleas, and we often scratch ourselves shamelessly; we have to ask permission to go to the latrines with humiliating frequency. Our wooden shoes are insupportably noisy and are plastered with alternate layers of mud and regulation grease.

Besides which, we are accustomed to our smell, but the girls are not and never miss a chance of showing it. It is not the generic smell of the badly washed, but the smell of the Häftling, faint and sweetish, which greeted us at our arrival in the Lager and which tenaciously pervades the dormitories, kitchens, washrooms and closets of the Lager. One acquires it at once and one never loses it: 'so young and already stinking!' is our way of greeting new arrivals.

To us the girls seem outside this world. There are three young German girls, Fräulein Liczba, the Polish storekeeper, and Frau Meyer, the secretary. They have smooth, rosy skin, beautiful attractive clothes, clean and warm, blond hair, long and well-set; they speak with grace and self-possession, and instead of keeping the Laboratory clean and in order, as they ought to, they smoke in the corners, scandalously eat bread and jam, file their nails, break a lot of glass vessels and then try to put the blame on us; when they sweep, they sweep our feet. They never speak to us and turn up their noses when they see us shuffling across the Laboratory, squalid and filthy, awkward and insecure in our shoes. I once asked Fräulein Liczba for some information, and she did not reply but turned with an annoyed face to Stawinoga and spoke to him quickly. I did not understand the sentence, but I clearly grasped '*Stinkjude*' and my blood froze. Stawinoga told me that for anything to do with the work we should turn directly to him.

These girls sing, like girls sing in laboratories all over the world, and it makes us deeply unhappy. They talk among themselves: they talk about the rationing, about their fiancés, about their homes, about the approaching holidays . . .

'Are you going home on Sunday? I am not, travelling is so uncomfortable!'

'I am going home for Christmas. Only two weeks and then it will be Christmas again; it hardly seems real, this year has gone by so quickly!'

. . . This year has gone by so quickly. This time last year I was a free man: an outlaw but free, I had a name and a family, I had an eager and restless mind, an agile and healthy body. I used to think of many, faraway things: of my work, of the end of the war, of good and evil, of the nature of things and of the laws which govern human actions; and also of the mountains, of singing and loving, of music, of poetry. I had an enormous, deep-rooted, foolish faith in the benevolence of fate; to kill and to die seemed extraneous literary things to me. My days were both cheerful and sad, but I regretted them equally, they were all full and positive; the future stood before me as a great treasure. Today the only thing left of the life of those days is what one needs to suffer hunger and cold; I am not even alive enough to know how to kill myself.

If I spoke German better I could try to explain all this to Frau Meyer; but she would certainly not understand, or if she was so good and intelligent as to understand, she would be unable to bear my proximity, and would flee from me, as one flees from contact with an incurable invalid, or from a man condemned to death. Or perhaps she would give me a coupon for a pint of civilian soup.

This year has gone by so quickly.

16 The Last One

By now Christmas is approaching. Alberto and I are walking side by side in the long grey file, bending forwards to resist the wind better. It is night and it is snowing; it is not easy to keep on one's feet, and even more difficult to keep up the pace in line; every now and again someone in front of us stumbles and falls in the black mud, and one has to be careful to avoid him and keep one's place in the column.

Since I started work in the Laboratory, Alberto and I work separately and we always have many things to tell each other on the return march. They are not usually things on a high level: about work, or our comrades, or the bread or the cold. But for a week now there had been something new: every evening Lorenzo brings us six or eight pints of soup from the Italian civilian workers. To solve the problem of transport, we had to procure what is called a '*menaschka*' here, that is, a zinc pot, made to order, more like a bucket than a pot. Silberlust, the tinsmith, made it for us from two scraps of a gutter in exchange for three rations of bread; it was a splendid, sturdy, capacious pitcher, with the characteristic shape of a neolithic tool.

In the whole camp there are only a few Greeks who have a *menaschka* larger than ours. Besides the material advantages, it carries with it a perceptible improvement in our social standing. A *menaschka* like ours is a diploma of nobility, a heraldic emblem: Henri is becoming our friend and speaks to us on equal terms; L. has assumed a paternal and condescending air; as for Elias, he is perpetually at our side, and although he spies on us with tenacity to discover the secret of our '*organisacja*', he overwhelms us at the same time with incomprehensible declarations of solidarity and affection, and deafens us with a litany of portentous obscenities and oaths in Italian and French which he learnt somewhere and by which he obviously means to honour us.

As for the moral aspect of the new state of affairs, Alberto and I are forced to agree that there is nothing to be very proud of; but it is so easy to find justifications! Besides, the very fact that we have new things to talk about is no negligible gain.

We talk about our plan to buy a second *menaschka* to rotate with the first, so that to make only one expedition a day to the remote corner of the yard where Lorenzo is now working will be sufficient. We speak about Lorenzo and how to reward him; later, if we return, we will of course do everything we can for him; but of what use is it to talk about that? He knows as well as us that we can hardly hope to return. We ought to do something at once; we could try to have his shoes repaired at the cobbler's shop in our Lager where repairs are free (it seems a paradox, but officially everything was free in the extermination camps). Alberto will try: he is a friend of the head cobbler, perhaps a few pints of soup will be enough.

We talk about three new exploits of ours, and we agree that for obvious reasons of professional secrecy it is inadvisable to talk about them at large: it is a pity, our personal prestige would be greatly increased.

As for the first, it is my brainchild. I knew that the *Blockältester* of Block 44 was short of brooms and I stole one in the yard; as far as this goes there is nothing extraordinary. The difficulty was to smuggle the broom into Lager on the return march, and I solved it in what I believe to be a completely original way: I took apart the handle and the head of the broom, sawing the former into two pieces and carrying the various parts separately into camp (the two pieces of the handle tied to my thighs inside my trousers) and then reconstructed the whole article. This required a piece of tin plate, a hammer and nails to join together the two pieces of wood. The whole business only took four days.

Contrary to what I feared, the customer not only did not devalue my broom but showed it as a curiosity to several of his friends, who gave me a regular order for two other brooms 'of the same model'.

But Alberto had other irons in the fire. In the first place he had put the finishing touches to 'Operation File' and had already carried it out successfully twice. Alberto goes to the tool-store, asks for a file and chooses a largish one. The storekeeper writes 'one file' next to his number and Alberto leaves. He goes straight to a safe civilian (a gem of a rascal from Trieste, as shrewd as they make them, who helps Alberto more for love of the art than for interest or philanthropy), who has no difficulty in exchanging the large file on the open market for two small ones of equal or lesser value. Alberto gives back 'one file' to the store and sells the other.

And he has just crowned his achievements with his masterpiece, an audacious new combination of singular elegance. It must first be stated that for some weeks now Alberto had been entrusted with a special duty: at the yard in the morning he is given a bucket with pliers, screwdrivers and several hundred celluloid labels in different colours, which he has to fit on to suitable clips in order to tag the numerous and lengthy pipes of hot and cold water, steam, compressed air, gas, naphtha, vacuum, etc. which run in all directions throughout the Polymerization Department. It must also be stated (and here there seems to be no connection: but does not ingenuity consist in the finding or creating of connections between apparently extraneous orders of ideas?) that for all us Häftlinge the shower constitutes a quite unpleasant occurrence for various reasons (the water is lacking and is cold or otherwise boiling, there is no changing-room, we have no towels nor soap, and during our enforced absence it is easy to be robbed). As the shower is obligatory, the *Blockältester* need a system of control enabling them to apply sanctions against whoever tries to evade it: usually a trusted member of the Block is placed at the door, and like Polyphemus touches everyone who comes out to feel if he is wet; if he is, he is given a ticket, if he is dry, he is given five blows from a truncheon. One can only claim one's bread the following morning by presenting the ticket.

Alberto's attention concentrated on the tickets. In general they are only wretched pieces of paper which are given back damp, crumpled and unrecognisable. Alberto knows his Germans and the *Blockältester* are all German, or German-trained: they love order, systems, bureaucracy; even more, although rough and irascible blockheads, they cherish an infantile delight in glittering, many-coloured objects.

Having played the theme, there follows the brilliant development. Alberto systematically withdrew a series of labels of the same colour; from each one he made three small discs (I organised the necessary instrument, a cork-borer, in the Laboratory): when two hundred discs were ready, enough for a Block, he went to the *Block-ältester* and offered him his '*Spezialität*' at the mad price of ten rations of bread, payment by instalments. The customer accepted with enthusiasm, and Alberto now has at his disposal a formidable article in fashion which is guaranteed to be accepted in every hut, one colour per hut: for no *Blockältester* wants to be regarded as niggardly or reactionary. Even more important, he has no need to be afraid of rivals, as he alone has access to the primary material. Is it not well thought out?

*

We talk about these things, stumbling from one puddle to the other, between the black of the sky and the mud of the road. We talk and we talk. I carry the two empty bowls, Alberto the happy weight of the full *menaschka*. Once again the music from the band, the ceremony of *'Mützen ab'*, hats smartly off in front of the SS; once more *'Arbeit Macht Frei'*, and the announcement of the Kapo: *'Kommando 98, zwei und sechzig Häftlinge, Stärke stimmt'*, sixty-two prisoners, number correct. But the column has not broken up, they have made a march as far as the roll-call square. Is there to be a roll-call? It is not a roll-call. We have seen the crude glare of the searchlight and the well-known profile of the gallows.

For more than an hour the squads continued to return, with the hard clatter of their wooden shoes on the frozen snow. When all the Kommandos had returned, the band suddenly stopped and a raucous German voice ordered silence. Another German voice rose up in the sudden quiet, and spoke for a long time angrily into the dark and hostile air. Finally the condemned man was brought out into the blaze of the searchlight.

All this pomp and ruthless ceremony are not new to us. I have already watched thirteen hangings since I entered the camp; but on the other occasions they were for ordinary crimes, thefts from the kitchen, sabotage, attempts to escape. Today it is different.

Last month one of the crematoria at Birkenau had been blown up. None of us knows (and perhaps no one will ever know) exactly how the exploit was carried out: there was talk of the *Sonderkommando*, the Special Kommando attached to the gas chambers and the ovens, which is itself periodically exterminated, and which is kept scrupulously segregated from the rest of the camp. The fact remains that a few hundred men at Birkenau, helpless and exhausted slaves like ourselves, had found in themselves the strength to act, to mature the fruits of their hatred.

The man who is to die in front of us today in some way took part in the revolt. They said he had contacts with the rebels of Birkenau, that he carried arms into our camp, that he was plotting a simultaneous mutiny among us. He is to die today before our very eyes: and perhaps the Germans do not understand that this solitary death, this man's death which has been reserved for him, will bring him glory, not infamy.

At the end of the German's speech, which nobody understood, the raucous voice of before again rose up: '*Habt ihr verstanden?*' (Have you understood?)

Who answered '*Jawohl*'? Everybody and nobody: it was as if our cursed resignation took body by itself, as if it turned into a collective voice above our heads. But everybody heard the cry of the doomed man, it pierced through the old thick barriers of inertia and submissiveness, it struck the living core of man in each of us:

'*Kamaraden, ich bin der Letz!*' (Comrades, I am the last one!).

I wish I could say that from the midst of us, an abject flock, a voice rose, a murmur, a sign of assent. But nothing happened. We remained standing, bent and grey, our heads dropped, and we did not uncover our heads until the German ordered us to do so. The trapdoor opened, the body wriggled horribly; the band began playing again and we were once more lined up and filed past the quivering body of the dying man.

At the foot of the gallows, the SS watch us pass with indifferent eyes: their work is finished, and well finished. The Russians can come now: there are no longer any strong men among us, the last one is now hanging above our heads, and as for the others, a few halters had been enough. The Russians can come now: they will only find us, the slaves, the worn-out, worthy of the unarmed death which awaits us.

To destroy a man is difficult, almost as difficult as to create one:

it has not been easy, nor quick, but you Germans have succeeded. Here we are, docile under your gaze; from our side you have nothing more to fear; no acts of violence, no words of defiance, not even a look of judgement.

Alberto and I went back to the hut, and we could not look each other in the face. That man must have been tough, he must have been made of another metal than us if this condition of ours, which has broken us, could not bend him.

Because we also are broken, conquered: even if we know how to adapt ourselves, even if we have finally learnt how to find our food and to resist the fatigue and cold, even if we return home.

We lifted the *menaschka* on to the bunk and divided it, we satisfied the daily ragings of hunger, and now we are oppressed by shame.

17 The Story of Ten Days

Already for some months now the distant booming of the Russian guns had been heard at intervals when, on 11 January 1945, I fell ill of scarlet fever and was once more sent into Ka-Be. '*Infektionsabteilung*': it meant a small room, really quite clean, with ten bunks on two levels, a wardrobe, three stools and a closet seat with the pail for corporal needs. All in a space of three yards by five.

It was difficult to climb to the upper bunks as there was no ladder; so, when a patient got worse, he was transferred to the lower bunks.

When I was admitted I was the thirteenth in the room. Four of the others – two French political prisoners and two young Hungarian Jews – had scarlet fever; there were three with diphtheria, two with typhus, while one suffered from a repellent facial erysipelas. The other two had more than one illness and were incredibly wasted away.

I had a high fever. I was lucky enough to have a bunk entirely to myself: I lay down with relief knowing that I had the right to forty days' isolation and therefore of rest, while I felt myself still sufficiently strong to fear neither the consequences of scarlet fever nor the selections.

Thanks to my by-now long experience of camp life I managed to bring with me all my personal belongings: a belt of interlaced electric wire, the knife-spoon, a needle with three needlefuls, five buttons and last of all eighteen flints which I had stolen from the Laboratory. From each of these, shaping them patiently with a knife, it was possible to make three smaller flints, just the right gauge for a normal cigarette lighter. They were valued at six or seven rations of bread.

I enjoyed four peaceful days. Outside it was snowing and very cold, but the room was heated. I was given strong doses of sulpha drugs, I suffered from an intense feeling of sickness and was hardly able to eat; I did not want to talk.

The two Frenchmen with scarlet fever were quite pleasant. They were provincials from the Vosges who had entered the camp only a few days before with a large convoy of civilians swept up by the Germans in their retreat from Lorraine. The elder one was named Arthur, a peasant, small and thin. The other, his bed-companion, was Charles, a schoolteacher, thirty-two years old; instead of a shirt he had been given a summer vest, ridiculously short.

On the fifth day the barber came. He was a Greek from Salonica: he spoke only the beautiful Spanish of his people, but understood some words of all the languages spoken in the camp. He was called Askenazi and had been in the camp for almost three years. I do not know how he managed to get the post of *Frisör* of Ka-Be: he spoke neither German nor Polish, nor was he in fact excessively brutal. Before he entered, I heard him speaking excitedly for a long time in the corridor with one of the doctors, a compatriot of his. He seemed to have an unusual look on his face, but as the expressions of the Levantines are different from ours, I could not tell whether he was afraid or happy or merely upset. He knew me, or at least knew that I was Italian.

When it was my turn I climbed down laboriously from the bunk. I asked him in Italian if there was anything new: he stopped shaving me, winked in a serious and allusive manner, pointed to the window with his chin, and then made a sweeping gesture with his hand towards the west.

'*Morgen, alle Kamarad weg.*'

He looked at me for a moment with his eyes wide open, as if waiting for a reaction, and then he added: '*todos, todos*' and returned to his work. He knew about my flints and shaved me with a certain gentleness.

The news excited no direct emotion in me. Already for many months I had no longer felt any pain, joy or fear, except in that detached and distant manner characteristic of the Lager, which might be described as conditional: if I still had my former sensitivity, I thought, this would be an extremely moving moment.

My ideas were perfectly clear; for a long time now Alberto and I had foreseen the dangers which would accompany the evacuation of the camp and the liberation. As for the rest, Askenazi's news was merely a confirmation of rumours which had been circulating for some days: that the Russians were at Censtochowa, sixty miles to the north; that they were at Zakopane, sixty miles to the south; that at Buna the Germans were already preparing the sabotage mines.

I looked at the faces of my comrades one by one: it was clearly useless to discuss it with any of them. They would have replied: 'Well?' and it would all have finished there. The French were different, they were still fresh.

'Did you hear?' I said to them. 'Tomorrow they are going to evacuate the camp.'

They overwhelmed me with questions. 'Where to? On foot? . . . The ill ones as well? Those who cannot walk?' They knew that I was an old prisoner and that I understood German, and deduced that I knew much more about the matter than I wanted to admit.

I did not know anything more: I told them so but they continued to ask questions. How stupid of them! But of course, they had only been in the Lager for a week and had not yet learnt that one did not ask questions.

In the afternoon the Greek doctor came. He said that all patients able to walk would be given shoes and clothes and would leave the following day with the healthy ones on a twelve-mile march. The others would remain in Ka-Be with assistants to be chosen from the patients least ill.

The doctor was unusually cheerful, he seemed drunk. I knew him: he was a cultured, intelligent man, egoistic and calculating. He added that everyone, without distinction, would receive a triple ration of bread, at which the patients visibly cheered up. We asked him what would happen to us. He replied that probably the Germans would leave us to our fate: no, he did not think that they would kill us. He made no effort to hide the fact that he thought otherwise. His very cheerfulness boded ill.

He was already equipped for the march. He had hardly gone out when the two Hungarian boys began to speak excitedly to each other. They were in an advanced state of convalescence but extremely wasted away. It was obvious that they were afraid to stay with the patients and were deciding to go with the healthy ones. It was not a question of reasoning: I would probably also have followed the instinct of the flock if I had not felt so weak; fear is supremely contagious, and its immediate reaction is to make one try to run away.

Outside the hut the camp sounded unusually excited. One of the two Hungarians got up, went out and returned half an hour later laden with filthy rags. He must have taken them from the storehouse of clothes still to be disinfected. He and his comrade dressed feverishly, putting on rag after rag. One could see that they were in a hurry to have the matter over with before the fear itself made them hesitate. It was crazy of them to think of walking even for one hour, weak as they were, especially in the snow with those broken-down shoes found at the last moment. I tried to explain, but they looked at me without replying. Their eyes were like those of terrified cattle.

Just for a moment it flashed through my mind that they might even be right. They climbed awkwardly out of the window; I saw them, shapeless bundles, lurching into the night. They did not return; I learnt much later that, unable to continue, they had been killed by the SS a few hours after the beginning of the march.

It was obvious that I, too, needed a pair of shoes. But it took me an hour to overcome the feeling of sickness, fever and inertia. I found a pair in the corridor. (The healthy prisoners had ransacked the deposit of patients' shoes and had taken the best ones; those remaining, with split soles and unpaired, lay all over the place.) Just then I met Kosman, the Alsatian. As a civilian he had been a Reuter correspondent at Clermont-Ferrand; he also was excited and euphoric. He said: 'If you return before me, write to the mayor of Metz that I am about to come back.'

Kosman was notorious for his acquaintances among the Prominents, so his optimism seemed a good sign and I used it to justify my inertia to myself; I hid the shoes and returned to bed.

Late that night the Greek doctor returned with a rucksack on his shoulders and a woollen hood. He threw a French novel on my bed. 'Keep it, read it, Italian. You can give it back to me when we meet again.' Even today I hate him for those words. He knew that we were doomed.

And then finally Alberto came, defying the prohibition, to say goodbye to me from the window. We were inseparable: we were 'the two Italians' and foreigners even mistook our names. For six months we had shared a bunk and every scrap of food 'organised' in excess of the ration; but he had had scarlet fever as a child and I was unable to infect him. So he left and I remained. We said goodbye, not many words were needed, we had already discussed our affairs countless times. We did not think we would be separated for very long. He had found a sturdy pair of leather shoes in a reasonable condition: he was one of those fellows who immediately find everything they need.

He also was cheerful and confident, as were all those who were leaving. It was understandable: something great and new was about to happen; we could finally feel a force around us which was not of Germany; we could concretely feel the impending collapse of that hated world of ours. At any rate, the healthy ones who, despite all their tiredness and hunger, were still able to move, could feel this. But it is obvious that whoever is too weak, or naked or barefoot, thinks and feels in a different way, and what dominated our thoughts was the paralysing sensation of being totally helpless in the hands of fate.

All the healthy prisoners (except a few prudent ones who at the last moment undressed and hid themselves in the hospital beds) left during the night of 18 January 1945. They must have been about twenty thousand, coming from different camps. Almost in their entirety they vanished during the evacuation march: Alberto was among them. Perhaps someone will write their story one day.

So we remained in our bunks, alone with our illnesses, and with our inertia stronger than fear.

In the whole Ka-Be we numbered perhaps eight hundred. In our room there were eleven of us, each in his own bunk, except for Charles and Arthur who slept together. The rhythm of the great machine of the Lager was extinguished. For us began the ten days outside both world and time.

18 January. During the night of the evacuation the camp kitchens continued to function, and on the following morning the last distribution of soup took place in the hospital. The central-heating plant had been abandoned; in the huts a little heat still lingered on, but hour by hour the temperature dropped and it was evident that we would soon suffer from the cold. Outside it must have been at least 5 °F below zero; most of the patients had only a shirt and some of them not even that.

Nobody knew what our fate would be. Some SS men had remained, some of the guard towers were still occupied.

About midday an SS officer made a tour of the huts. He appointed a chief in each of them, selecting from among the remaining non-Jews, and ordered a list of the patients to be made at once, divided into Jews and non-Jews. The matter seemed clear. No one was surprised that the Germans preserved their national love of classification until the very end, nor did any Jew seriously expect to live until the following day.

The two Frenchmen had not understood and were frightened. I translated the speech of the SS man. I was annoyed that they should be afraid: they had not even experienced a month of the Lager, they hardly suffered from hunger yet, they were not even Jews, but they were afraid.

There was one more distribution of bread. I spent the afternoon reading the book left by the doctor: it was interesting and I can remember it with curious accuracy. I also made a visit to the neighbouring ward in search of blankets; many patients had been sent out from there and their blankets were free. I brought back some quite heavy ones.

When Arthur heard that they came from the dysentery ward, he looked disgusted: '*Y avait point besoin de le dire*'; in fact, they were polluted. But I thought that in any case, knowing what awaited us, we might as well sleep comfortably.

It was soon night but the electric light remained on. We saw with tranquil fear that an armed SS man stood at the corner of the hut. I had no desire to talk and was not afraid except in that external and conditional manner I have described. I continued reading until late.

There were no clocks, but it must have been about 11 p.m. when all the lights went out, even those of the reflectors on the guard towers. One could see the searchlight beams in the distance. A cluster of intense lights burst out in the sky, remaining immobile, crudely illuminating the earth. One could hear the roar of the aeroplanes.

Then the bombardment began. It was nothing new: I climbed down to the ground, put my bare feet into my shoes and waited.

It seemed far away, perhaps over Auschwitz.

But then there was an explosion near by, and before one could think, a second and a third one, loud enough to burst one's eardrums. Windows were breaking, the hut shook, the spoon I had fixed in the wall fell down.

Then it seemed all over. Cagnolati, a young peasant also from the Vosges, had apparently never experienced a raid. He had jumped out naked from his bed and was concealed in a corner, screaming. After a few minutes it was obvious that the camp had been struck. Two huts were burning fiercely, another two had been pulverised, but they were all empty. Dozens of patients arrived, naked and wretched, from a hut threatened by fire: they asked for shelter. It was impossible to take them in. They insisted, begging and threatening in many languages. We had to barricade the door. They dragged themselves elsewhere, lit up by the flames, barefoot in the melting snow. Many trailed behind them streaming bandages. There seemed no danger to our hut, so long as the wind did not change.

The Germans were no longer there. The towers were empty.

*

Today I think that if for no other reason than that an Auschwitz existed, no one in our age should speak of Providence. But without doubt in that hour the memory of biblical salvations in times of extreme adversity passed like a wind through all our minds.

It was impossible to sleep; a window was broken and it was very cold. I was thinking that we would have to find a stove to set up and get some coal, wood and food. I knew that it was all essential, but without some help I would never have had the energy to carry it out. I spoke about it to the two Frenchmen.

19 January. The Frenchmen agreed. We got up at dawn, we three. I felt ill and helpless, I was cold and afraid.

The other patients looked at us with respectful curiosity: did we not know that patients were not allowed to leave Ka-Be? And if the Germans had not all left? But they said nothing, they were glad that someone was prepared to make the test.

The Frenchmen had no idea of the topography of the Lager, but Charles was courageous and robust, while Arthur was shrewd, with the practical common sense of the peasant. We went out into the wind of a freezing day of fog, poorly wrapped up in blankets.

What we saw resembled nothing that I had ever seen or heard described.

The Lager, hardly dead, had already begun to decompose. No more water, or electricity, broken windows and doors slamming to in the wind, loose iron-sheets from the roofs screeching, ashes from the fire drifting high, afar. The work of the bombs had been completed by the work of man: ragged, decrepit, skeleton-like patients at all able to move dragged themselves everywhere on the frozen soil, like an invasion of worms. They had ransacked all the empty huts in search of food and wood; they had violated with senseless fury the grotesquely adorned rooms of the hated *Block-*

ältester, forbidden to the ordinary Häftlinge until the previous day;
no longer in control of their own bowels, they had fouled everywhere, polluting the precious snow, the only source of water
remaining in the whole camp.

Around the smoking ruins of the burnt huts, groups of patients
lay stretched out on the ground, soaking up its last warmth. Others
had found potatoes somewhere and were roasting them on the
embers of the fire, glaring around with fierce eyes. A few had had
the strength to light a real fire, and were melting snow in it in any
handy receptacle.

We hurried to the kitchens as fast as we could; but the potatoes
were almost finished. We filled two sacks and left them in Arthur's
keeping. Among the ruins of the *Prominenzblock* Charles and I
finally found what we were searching for: a heavy cast-iron stove,
with the flue still usable. Charles hurried over with a wheelbarrow
and we loaded it on; he then left me with the task of carrying it to
the hut and ran back to the sacks. There he found Arthur unconscious from the cold. Charles picked up both sacks and carried
them to safety, then he took care of his friend.

Meanwhile, staggering with difficulty, I was trying to man-
oeuvre the heavy wheelbarrow as best I could. There was the roar
of an engine and an SS man entered the camp on a motor cycle. As
always when I saw their hard faces I froze from terror and hatred.
It was too late to disappear and I did not want to abandon the
stove. The rules of the Lager stated that one must stand to attention with head uncovered. I had no hat and was encumbered by
the blanket. I moved a few steps away from the wheelbarrow and
made a sort of awkward bow. The German moved on without seeing me, turned behind a hut and left. Only later did I realise the
danger I had run.

I finally reached the entrance of the hut and unloaded the stove into Charles's hands. I was completely breathless from the effort, large black spots danced before my eyes.

It was essential to get it working. We all three had our hands paralysed while the icy metal stuck to the skin of our fingers, but it was vitally urgent to set it up to warm ourselves and to boil the potatoes. We had found wood and coal as well as embers from the burnt huts.

When the broken window was repaired and the stove began to spread its heat, something seemed to relax in everyone, and at that moment Towarowski (a Franco-Pole of twenty-three, typhus) proposed to the others that each of them offer a slice of bread to us three who had been working. And so it was agreed.

Only a day before a similar event would have been inconceivable. The law of the Lager said: 'eat your own bread, and if you can, that of your neighbour', and left no room for gratitude. It really meant that the Lager was dead.

It was the first human gesture that occurred among us. I believe that that moment can be dated as the beginning of the change by which we who had not died slowly turned from Häftlinge to men again.

Arthur recovered quite well, but from then on always avoided exposing himself to the cold; he undertook the upkeep of the stove, the cooking of the potatoes, the cleaning of the room and the helping of the patients. Charles and I shared the various tasks outside. There was still an hour of light: an expedition yielded us a pint of spirits and a tin of yeast, thrown in the snow by someone; we made a distribution of potatoes and one spoonful of yeast per person. I thought vaguely that it might help against lack of vitamins.

Darkness fell; in the whole camp ours was the only room with a stove, of which we were very proud. Many invalids from other wards crowded around the door, but Charles's imposing stature held them back. Nobody, neither us nor them, thought that the inevitable promiscuity with our patients made it extremely dangerous to stay in our room, and to fall ill of diphtheria in those conditions was more surely fatal than jumping off a fourth floor.

I myself was aware of it, but I did not dwell long on the idea: for too long I had been accustomed to think of death by illness as a possible event, and in that case unavoidable, and anyhow beyond any possible intervention on our part. And it did not even pass through my mind that I could have gone to another room in another hut with less danger of infection. The stove, our creation, was here, and spread a wonderful warmth; I had my bed here; and by now a tie united us, the eleven patients of the *Infektionsabteilung.*

Very occasionally we heard the thundering of artillery, both near and far, and at intervals the crackling of automatic rifles. In the darkness, lighted only by the glow of the embers, Arthur and I sat smoking cigarettes made of herbs found in the kitchen, and spoke of many things, both past and future. In the middle of this endless plain, frozen and full of war, in the small dark room swarming with germs, we felt at peace with ourselves and with the world. We were broken by tiredness, but we seemed to have finally accomplished something useful – perhaps like God after the first day of creation.

20 January. The dawn came and it was my turn to light the stove. Besides a general feeling of weakness, the aching of my joints reminded me all the time that my scarlet fever was far from over. The thought of having to plunge into the freezing air to find a light in the other huts made me shudder with disgust. I remembered my flints: I sprinkled a piece of paper with spirits, and patiently scraped a small pile of black dust on top of it and then scraped the flint more vigorously with my knife. And finally, after a few sparks, the small pile caught fire and the small bluish flame of alcohol rose from the paper.

Arthur climbed down enthusiastically from his bed and heated three potatoes per person from those boiled the day before; after which, Charles and I, starved and shivering violently, left again to explore the decaying camp.

We had enough food (that is, potatoes) for two days only; as for water, we were forced to melt the snow, an awkward operation in the absence of large pots, which yielded a blackish, muddy liquid which had to be filtered.

The camp was silent. Other starving spectres like ourselves wandered around searching, unshaven, with hollow eyes, greyish skeleton bones in rages. Shaky on their legs, they entered and left the empty huts carrying the most varied of objects: axes, buckets, ladles, nails; anything might be of use, and those looking furthest ahead were already thinking of profitable commerce with the Poles of the surrounding countryside.

In the kitchen we found two of them squabbling over the last handfuls of putrid potatoes. They had seized each other by their rags, and were fighting with curiously slow and uncertain movements, cursing in Yiddish between their frozen lips.

In the courtyard of the storehouse there were two large piles of cabbages and turnips (those large, insipid turnips, the basis of our diet). They were so frozen that they could only be separated with a pickaxe. Charles and I took turns, using all our energy at each stroke, and we carried out about 100 pounds. There was still more: Charles discovered a packet of salt and (*'Une fameuse trouvaille!'*) a can of water of perhaps twelve gallons, frozen in a block.

We loaded everything on to a small cart (formerly used to distribute the rations for the huts; there were a great number of them abandoned everywhere), and we turned back, toiling over the snow.

We contented ourselves that day with boiled potatoes again and slices of turnips roasted on the stove, but Arthur promised important innovations for the following day.

In the afternoon I went to the ex-surgery, searching for anything that might prove of use. I had been preceded: everything had been upset by inexpert looters. Not a bottle intact, the floor covered by a layer of rags, excrement and soiled bandages. A naked, contorted corpse. But there was something that had escaped my predecessors: a battery from a lorry. I touched the poles with a knife – a small spark. It was charged.

That evening we had light in our room.

Sitting in bed, I could see a large stretch of the road through the window. For the past three days the Wehrmacht in flight passed by in waves. Armoured cars, Tiger tanks camouflaged in white, Germans on horseback, Germans on bicycles, Germans on foot, armed and unarmed. During the night, long before the tanks came into sight, one could hear the grinding of their tracks.

Charles asked: '*Ça roule encore?*'

'*Ça roule toujours.*'

It seemed as if it would never end.

21 *January.* Instead it ended. On the dawn of the 21st we saw the plain deserted and lifeless, white as far as the eye could see, lying under the flight of the crows, deathly sad. I would almost have preferred to see something moving again. The Polish civilians had also disappeared, hiding who knows where. Even the wind seemed to have stopped. I wanted only one thing: to stay in bed under my blankets and abandon myself to a complete exhaustion of muscles, nerve and will-power; waiting as indifferently as a dead man for it to end or not to end.

But Charles had already lighted the stove, Charles, our active, trusting, alive friend, and he called me to work:

'*Vas-y, Primo, descends-toi de là-haut; il y a Jules à attraper par les oreilles . . .*'

'Jules' was the lavatory bucket, which every morning had to be taken by its handles, carried outside and emptied into the cesspool; this was the first task of the day, and if one remembers that it was impossible to wash one's hands and that three of us were ill with typhus, it can be understood that it was not a pleasant job.

We had to inaugurate the cabbages and turnips. While I went to search for wood and Charles collected the snow for water, Arthur mobilised the patients who could sit up to help with the peeling. Towarowski, Sertelet, Alcalai and Schenck answered the call.

Sertelet was also a peasant from the Vosges, twenty years old; he seemed in good shape, but day by day his voice assumed an ever more sinister nasal timbre, reminding us that diphtheria seldom relaxes its hold.

Alcalai was a Jewish glazier from Toulouse; he was quiet and discreet, and suffered from erysipelas on the face.

Schenck was a Slovak businessman, Jewish; a typhus patient, he had a formidable appetite. Likewise Towarowski, a Franco-Polish Jew, stupid and talkative, but useful to our community through his communicative optimism.

So while the patients scraped with their knives, each one seated on his bunk, Charles and I devoted ourselves to finding a suitable site for the kitchen operations. An indescribable filth had invaded every part of the camp. All the latrines were overflowing, as naturally nobody cared any more about their upkeep, and those suffering from dysentery (more than a hundred) had fouled every corner of Ka-Be, filling all the buckets, all the bowls formerly used for the rations, all the pots. One could not move an inch without watching one's step; in the dark it was impossible to move around. Although suffering from the cold, which remained acute, we thought with horror of what would happen if it thawed: the diseases would spread irreparably, the stench would be suffocating, and even more, with the snow melted we would remain definitively without water.

After a long search we finally found a small area of floor not excessively soiled in a spot formerly used for the laundry. We lit a live fire to save time and complications and disinfected our hands, rubbing them with chloramine mixed with snow.

The news that a soup was being cooked spread rapidly through the crowd of the semi-living; a throng of starved faces gathered at the door. Charles, with ladle uplifted, made a short, vigorous speech, which although in French needed no translation.

The majority dispersed but one came forward. He was a Parisian, a high-class tailor (he said), suffering from tuberculosis. In exchange for two pints of soup he offered to make us clothes from the many blankets still to be found in the camp.

Maxime showed himself really able. The following day Charles and I were in possession of a jacket, trousers and gloves of a rough fabric of striking colours.

In the evening, after the first soup, distributed with enthusiasm and devoured with greed, the great silence of the plain was broken. From our bunks, too tired to be really worried, we listened to the bangs of mysterious artillery groups apparently hidden on all the points of the horizon, and to the whistle of the shells over our heads.

I was thinking life outside was beautiful and would be beautiful again, and that it would really be a pity to let ourselves be overcome now. I woke up the patients who were dozing and when I was sure that they were all listening I told them, first in French and then in my best German, that they must all begin to think of returning home now, and that as far as depended on us, certain things were to be done and others to be avoided. Each person should carefully look after his own bowl and spoon; no one should offer his own soup to others; no one should climb down from his bed except to go to the latrine; if anyone was in need of anything, he should only turn to us three. Arthur in particular was given the task of supervising the discipline and hygiene, and was to remember that it was better to leave bowls and spoons dirty rather than wash them with the danger of changing those of a diphtheria patient with those of someone suffering from typhus.

I had the impression that the patients by now were too indifferent to everything to pay attention to what I had said; but I had great faith in Arthur's diligence.

22 January. If it is courageous to face a grave danger with a light heart, Charles and I were courageous that morning. We extended our explorations to the SS camp, immediately outside the electric wire-fence.

The camp guards must have left in a great hurry. On the tables we found plates half-full of a by-now frozen soup which we devoured with an intense pleasure, mugs full of beer, transformed into a yellowish ice, a chessboard with an unfinished game. In the dormitories, piles of valuable things.

We loaded ourselves with a bottle of vodka, various medicines, newspapers and magazines and four first-rate eiderdowns, one of which is today in my house in Turin. Cheerful and irresponsible, we carried the fruits of our expedition back to the dormitory, leaving them in Arthur's care. Only that evening did we learn what happened perhaps only half an hour later.

Some SS men, perhaps dispersed, but still armed, penetrated

into the abandoned camp. They found that eighteen Frenchmen
had settled in the dining-hall of the SS-Waffe. They killed them all
methodically, with a shot in the nape of the neck, lining up their
twisted bodies in the snow on the road; then they left. The eighteen
corpses remained exposed until the arrival of the Russians; nobody
had the strength to bury them.

But by now there were beds in all the huts occupied by corpses
as rigid as wood, whom nobody troubled to remove. The ground
was too frozen to dig graves; many bodies were piled up in a trench,
but already early on the heap showed out of the hole and was
shamefully visible from our window.

Only a wooden wall separated us from the ward of the dysentery patients, where many were dying and many dead. The floor
was covered by a layer of frozen excrement. None of the patients
had strength enough to climb out of their blankets to search for
food, and those who had done it at the beginning had not returned
to help their comrades. In one bed, clasping each other to resist the
cold better, there were two Italians. I often heard them talking, but
as I spoke only French, for a long time they were not aware of my
presence. That day they heard my name by chance, pronounced
with an Italian accent by Charles, and from then on they never
ceased groaning and imploring.

Naturally I would have liked to have helped them, given the
means and the strength, if for no other reason than to stop their
crying. In the evening when all the work was finished, conquering
my tiredness and disgust, I dragged myself gropingly along the
dark, filthy corridor to their ward with a bowl of water and the
remainder of our day's soup. The result was that from then on,
through the thin wall, the whole diarrhoea ward shouted my name
day and night with the accents of all the languages of Europe,
accompanied by incomprehensible prayers, without my being able

to do anything about it. I felt like crying, I could have cursed them.

The night held ugly surprises.

Lakmaker, in the bunk under mine, was a poor wreck of a man. He was (or had been) a Dutch Jew, seventeen years old, tall, thin and gentle. He had been in bed for three months; I have no idea how he had managed to survive the selections. He had had typhus and scarlet fever successively; at the same time a serious cardiac illness had shown itself, while he was smothered with bedsores, so much so that by now he could only lie on his stomach. Despite all this, he had a ferocious appetite. He only spoke Dutch, and none of us could understand him.

Perhaps the cause of it all was the cabbage-and-turnip soup, of which Lakmaker had wanted two helpings. In the middle of the night he groaned and then threw himself from his bed. He tried to reach the latrine, but was too weak and fell to the ground, crying and shouting loudly.

Charles lit the lamp (the battery showed itself providential) and we were able to ascertain the gravity of the incident. The boy's bed and the floor were filthy. The smell in the small area was rapidly becoming insupportable. We had but a minimum supply of water and neither blankets nor straw mattresses to spare. And the poor wretch, suffering from typhus, formed a terrible source of infection, while he could certainly not be left all night to groan and shiver in the cold in the middle of the filth.

Charles climbed down from his bed and dressed in silence. While I held the lamp, he cut all the dirty patches from the straw mattress and the blankets with a knife. He lifted Lakmaker from the ground with the tenderness of a mother, cleaned him as best as possible with straw taken from the mattress and lifted him into the remade bed in the only position in which the unfortunate fellow could lie. He scraped the floor with a scrap of tin plate, diluted a little chloramine and finally spread disinfectant over everything, including himself.

I judged his self-sacrifice by the tiredness which I would have had to overcome in myself to do what he had done.

23 January. Our potatoes were finished. For days past the rumour had circulated through all the huts that an enormous trench of potatoes lay somewhere outside the barbed wire, not far from the camp.

Some unknown pioneer must have carried out patient explorations, or else someone knew the spot with precision. In fact, by the morning of the 23rd a section of the barbed wire had been beaten down and a double file of wretches went in and out through the opening.

Charles and I left, into the wind of the leaden plain. We were beyond the broken barrier.

'*Dis donc, Primo, on est dehors!*'

It was exactly like that; for the first time since the day of my arrest I found myself free, without armed guards, without wire fences between myself and home.

Perhaps 400 yards from the camp lay the potatoes – a treasure. Two extremely long ditches, full of potatoes and covered by alternate layers of soil and straw to protect them from the cold. Nobody would die of hunger any more.

But to extract them was by no means easy work. The cold had made the surface of the earth as hard as iron. By strenuous work with a pickaxe it was possible to break the crust and lay bare the supply; but the majority preferred to work the holes abandoned by others and continue to deepen them, passing the potatoes to their companions standing outside.

An old Hungarian had been surprised there by death. He lay there like hunger personified: head and shoulders under a pile of earth, belly in the snow, hands stretched out towards the potatoes. Someone came later and moved the body about a yard, so freeing the hole.

From then on our food improved. Besides boiled potatoes and potato soup, we offered our patients potato pancakes, on Arthur's recipe: rub together raw potatoes with boiled, soft ones, and roast the mixture on a red-hot iron plate. They tasted of soot.

But Sertelet, steadily getting worse, was unable to enjoy them. Besides speaking with an ever more nasal tone, that day he was unable to force down any food; something had closed up in his throat, every mouthful threatened to suffocate him.

I went to look for a Hungarian doctor left as a patient in the hut in front. When he heard the word diphtheria he started back and ordered me to leave.

For pure propaganda purposes I gave everyone nasal drops of camphorated oil. I assured Sertelet that they would help him; I even tried to convince myself.

24 January. Liberty. The breach in the barbed wire gave us a concrete image of it. To anyone who stopped to think, it signified no more Germans, no more selections, no work, no blows, no roll-calls, and perhaps, later, the return.

But we had to make an effort to convince ourselves of it, and no one had time to enjoy the thought. All around lay destruction and death.

The pile of corpses in front of our window had by now overflowed out of the ditch. Despite the potatoes everyone was extremely weak: not a patient in the camp improved, while many fell ill with pneumonia and diarrhoea; those who were unable to move themselves, or lacked the energy to do so, lay lethargic in their bunks, benumbed by the cold, and nobody realised when they died.

The others were all incredibly tired: after months and years of the Lager it needs more than potatoes to give back strength to a man. Charles and I, as soon as we had dragged the fifty pints of daily soup from the laundry to our room, threw ourselves panting on the bunks, while Arthur, with that domesticated air of his, diligently divided the food, taking care to save the three rations of '*rabiot pour les travailleurs*' and a little of the sediment '*pour les Italiens d'à côté*'.

In the second room of the contagious ward, likewise adjoining ours and occupied mainly by tuberculosis patients, the situation was quite different. All those who were able to had gone to other huts. Their weakest comrades and those who were most seriously ill died one by one in solitude.

I went in there one morning to try and borrow a needle. A patient was wheezing in one of the upper bunks. He heard me, struggled to sit up, then fell dangling, head downwards over the edge towards me, with his chest and arms stiff and his eyes white. The man in the bunk below automatically stretched up his arms to support the body and then realised that he was dead. He slowly withdrew from under the weight and the body slid to the ground where it remained. Nobody knew his name.

But in hut 14 something new had happened. It was occupied by patients recovering from operations, some of them quite healthy. They organised an expedition to the English prisoner-of-war camp, which it was assumed had been evacuated. It proved a fruitful expedition. They returned dressed in khaki with a cart full of wonders never seen before: margarine, custard powders, lard, soyabean flour, whisky.

That evening there was singing in hut 14.

None of us felt strong enough to walk the one mile to the

English camp and return with a load. But indirectly the fortunate expedition proved of advantage to many. The unequal division of goods caused a reflourishing of industry and commerce. Our room, with its lethal atmosphere, transformed itself into a factory of candles poured into cardboard moulds, with wicks soaked in boracic acid. The riches of hut 14 absorbed our entire production, paying us in lard and flour.

I myself had found the block of beeswax in the *Elektromagazin*; I remember the expression of disappointment of those who saw me carry it away and the dialogue that followed:

'What do you want to do with that?'

It was inadvisable to reveal a shop secret; I heard myself replying with the words I had often heard spoken by the old ones of the camp, expressing their favourite boast – of being hard-boiled, 'old hands', who always knew how to find their feet: '*Ich verstehe verschiedene Sachen.*' I know how to do many things . . .

25 January. It was Sómogyi's turn. He was a Hungarian chemist, about fifty years old, thin, tall and taciturn. Like the Dutchman he suffered from typhus and scarlet fever. He had not spoken for perhaps five days; that day he opened his mouth and said in a firm voice:

'I have a ration of bread under the sack. Divide it among you three. I shall not be eating any more.'

We could not find anything to say, but for the time being we did not touch the bread. Half his face had swollen. As long as he retained consciousness he remained closed in a harsh silence.

But in the evening and for the whole of the night and for two days without interruption the silence was broken by his delirium. Following a last interminable dream of acceptance and slavery he began to murmur: '*Jawohl*' with every breath, regularly and continuously like a machine, '*Jawohl* ', at every collapsing of his wretched frame, thousands of times, enough to make one want to shake him, to suffocate him, at least to make him change the word.

I never understood so clearly as at that moment how laborious is the death of a man.

Outside the great silence continued. The number of ravens had increased considerably and everybody knew why. Only at distant intervals did the dialogue of the artillery wake up.

We all said to each other that the Russians would arrive soon, at once; we all proclaimed it, we were all sure of it, but at bottom nobody believed it. Because one loses the habit of hoping in the Lager, and even of believing in one's own reason. In the Lager it is useless to think, because events happen for the most part in an unforeseeable manner; and it is harmful, because it keeps alive a sensitivity which is a source of pain, and which some providential natural law dulls when suffering passes a certain limit.

Like joy, fear and pain itself, even expectancy can be tiring. Having reached 25 January, with all relations broken already for eight days with that ferocious world that still remained a world, most of us were too exhausted even to wait.

In the evening, around the stove, Charles, Arthur and I felt ourselves become men once again. We could speak of everything. I grew enthusiastic at Arthur's account of how one passed the Sunday at Provenchères in the Vosges, and Charles almost cried when I told him the story of the armistice in Italy, of the turbid and desperate beginning of the Partisan resistance, of the man who betrayed us and of our capture in the mountains.

In the darkness, behind and above us, the eight invalids did not lose a syllable, even those who did not understand French. Only Sómogyi implacably confirmed his dedication to death.

*

26 January. We lay in a world of death and phantoms. The last trace of civilisation had vanished around and inside us. The work of bestial degradation, begun by the victorious Germans, had been carried to its conclusion by the Germans in defeat.

It is man who kills, man who creates or suffers injustice; it is no longer man who, having lost all restraint, shares his bed with a corpse. Whoever waits for his neighbour to die in order to take his piece of bread is, albeit guiltless, further from the model of thinking man than the most primitive pygmy or the most vicious sadist.

Part of our existence lies in the feelings of those near to us. This is why the experience of someone who has lived for days during which man was merely a thing in the eyes of man is non-human. We three were for the most part immune from it, and we owe each other mutual gratitude. This is why my friendship with Charles will prove lasting.

But thousands of feet above us, in the gaps in the grey clouds, the complicated miracles of aerial duels began. Above us, bare, helpless and unarmed, men of our time sought reciprocal death with the most refined of instruments. A movement of a finger could cause the destruction of the entire camp, could annihilate thousands of men; while the sum total of all our efforts and exertions would not be sufficient to prolong by one minute the life of even one of us.

The saraband stopped at night and the room was once again filled with Sómogyi's monologue.

In full darkness I found myself suddenly awake. '*L' pauv' vieux*' was silent; he had finished. With the last gasp of life, he had thrown himself to the ground: I heard the thud of his knees, of his hips, of his shoulders, of his head.

'*La mort l'a chassé de son lit,*' Arthur defined it.

We certainly could not carry him out during the night. There was nothing for it but to go back to sleep again.

27 January. Dawn. On the floor, the shameful wreck of skin and bones, the Sómogyi thing.

There are more urgent tasks: we cannot wash ourselves, so that we dare not touch him until we have cooked and eaten. And besides: '. . . *rien de si dégoûtant que les débordements,*' said Charles justly; the latrine had to be emptied. The living are more demanding; the dead can wait. We began to work as on every day.

The Russians arrived while Charles and I were carrying Sómogyi a little distance outside. He was very light. We overturned the stretcher on the grey snow.

Charles took off his beret. I regretted not having a beret.

Of the eleven of the *Infektionsabteilung* Sómogyi was the only one to die in the ten days. Sertelet, Cagnolati, Towarowski, Lakmaker and Dorget (I have not spoken of him so far; he was a French industrialist who, after an operation for peritonitis, fell ill of nasal diphtheria) died some weeks later in the temporary Russian hospital of Auschwitz. In April, at Katowice, I met Schenck and Alcalai in good health. Arthur has reached his family happily and Charles has taken up his teacher's profession again; we have exchanged long letters and I hope to see him again one day.

Afterword: The Author's Answers to His Readers' Questions

Someone a long time ago wrote that books too, like human beings, have their destiny: unpredictable, different from what is desired and expected. This book also has a strange destiny. Its birth certificate is distant: it can be found where one reads that 'I write what I would never dare tell anyone.' My need to tell the story was so strong in the camp that I had begun describing my experiences there, on the spot, in that German laboratory laden with freezing cold, the war, and vigilant eyes; and yet I knew that I would not be able under any circumstances to hold on to those haphazardly scribbled notes, and that I must throw them away immediately because if they were found they would be considered an act of espionage and would cost me my life.

Nevertheless, those memories burned so intensely inside me that I felt compelled to write as soon as I returned to Italy, and within a few months I wrote *If This Is a Man*. The manuscript was turned down by a number of important publishers; it was accepted in 1947 by a small publisher who printed only 2,500 copies and then folded. So this first book of mine fell into oblivion for many years: perhaps also because in all of Europe those were difficult times of mourning and reconstruction and the public did not want to return in memory to the painful years of the war that had just ended. It achieved a new life only in 1958, when it was republished by Einaudi, and from then on the interest of the public has never flagged. In Italy the book has sold more than 500,000 copies; it has been translated into eight languages and adapted for radio and the theatre. This belated success encouraged me to write *The Truce*, the natural continuation of its older brother, which, unlike it, immediately met with an excellent reception from the public and critics.

In the course of the years, I have been asked to comment on the two books hundreds of times, before the most diverse audiences: young and adult, uneducated and cultivated, in Italy and abroad. On the occasion of these encounters, I have had to answer many questions: naïve, acute, highly emotional, superficial, at times provocative. I soon realised that some of these questions recurred constantly; indeed, never failed to be asked: they must therefore spring from a thoughful curiosity, to which in some way the text of the book did not give a satisfactory reply. I propose to reply to these questions here.

1. In these books there are no expressions of hate for the Germans, no desire for revenge. Have you forgiven them?
My personal temperament is not inclined to hatred. I regard it as bestial, crude, and prefer on the contrary that my actions and thoughts, as far as possible, should be the product of reason; therefore I have never cultivated within myself hatred as a desire for revenge, or as a desire to inflict suffering on my real or presumed enemy, or as a private vendetta. Even less do I accept hatred as directed collectively at an ethnic group, for example, all the Germans; if I accepted it, I would feel that I was following the precepts of Nazism, which was founded precisely on national and racial hatred.

I must admit that if I had in front of me one of our persecutors of those days, certain known faces, certain old lies, I would be tempted to hate, and with violence too; but exactly because I am not a Fascist or a Nazi, I refuse to give way to this temptation. I believe in reason and in discussion as supreme instruments of progress, and therefore I repress hatred even within myself: I prefer justice. Precisely for this reason, when describing the tragic world of Auschwitz, I have deliberately assumed the calm, sober language of the witness, neither the lamenting tones of the victim nor the irate voice of someone who seeks revenge. I thought that my account would be all the more credible and useful the more it appeared objective and the less it sounded overly emotional; only in this way does a witness in matters of justice perform his task, which is that of preparing the ground for the judge. The judges are my readers.

All the same I would not want my abstaining from explicit judgement to be confused with an indiscriminate pardon. No, I have not forgiven any of the culprits, nor am I willing to forgive a single one of them, unless he has shown (with deeds, not words, and not too long afterwards) that he has become conscious of the crimes and errors of Italian and foreign Fascism and is determined to condemn them, uproot them, from his conscience and from that of others. Only in this case am I, a non-Christian, prepared to follow the Jewish and Christian precept of forgiving my enemy, because an enemy who sees the error of his ways ceases to be an enemy.

2. Did the Germans know what was happening?
How is it possible that the extermination of millions of human beings could have been carried out in the heart of Europe without anyone's knowledge?

The world in which we Westerners live has grave faults and dangers, but when compared to the countries in which democracy is smothered, and to the times during which it has been smothered, our world has a tremendous advantage: everyone can know everything about everything. Information today is the 'fourth estate': at least in theory the reporter, the journalist and the news photographer have free access everywhere; nobody has the right to stop them or send them away. Everything is easy: if you wish you can receive radio or television broadcasts from your own country or from any other country. You can go to the news-stand and choose the newspaper you prefer, national or foreign, of any political tendency – even that of a country with which your country is at odds. You can buy and read any books you want and usually do not risk being incriminated for 'antinational activity' or bring down on your house a search by the political police. Certainly it is not easy to avoid all biases, but at least you can pick the bias you prefer.

In an authoritarian state it is not like this. There is only one Truth, proclaimed from above; the newspapers are all alike, they all repeat the same one Truth. So do the radio stations, and you cannot listen to those of other countries. In the first place, since this is a crime, you risk ending up in prison. In the second place, the radio stations in your country send out jamming signals, on the appropriate wavelengths, that superimpose themselves on the foreign messages and prevent your hearing them. As for books, only those that please the State are published and translated. You must seek any others on the outside and introduce them into your country at your own risk because they are considered more dangerous than drugs and explosives, and if they are found in your possession at the border, they are confiscated and you are punished. Books not in favour, or no longer in favour, are burned in public bonfires in town squares. This went on in Italy between 1924 and 1945; it went on in National Socialist Germany; it is going on right now in many countries, among which it is sad to have to number the Soviet Union, which fought heroically against Fascism. In an authoritarian State it is considered permissible to alter the truth; to rewrite history retrospectively; to distort the news, suppress the true, add the false. Propaganda is substituted for information. In fact, in such a country you are not a citizen possessor of rights but a subject, and as such you owe to the State (and to the dictator who represents it) fanatical loyalty and supine obedience.

It is clear that under these conditions it becomes possible (though not always easy; it is never easy to deeply violate human nature) to erase great chunks of reality. In Fascist Italy the undertaking to assassinate the Socialist deputy Matteotti was quite successful, and after a few months it was locked in silence. Hitler and his Minister of Propaganda, Joseph Goebbels, showed themselves to be far superior to Mussolini at this work of controlling and masking truth.

However, it was not possible to hide the existence of the enormous concentration-camp apparatus from the German people. What's more, it was not (from the Nazi point of view) even desirable. Creating and maintaining an atmosphere of undefined terror in the country was part of the aims of Nazism. It was just as well for the people to know that opposing Hitler was extremely dangerous. In fact, hundreds of thousands of Germans were confined in the camps from the very first months of Nazism: Communists, Social Democrats, Liberals, Jews, Protestants, Catholics; the whole country knew it and knew that in the camps people were suffering and dying.

Nevertheless, it is true that the great mass of Germans remained unaware of the most atrocious details of what happened later on in the camps: the methodical industrialised extermination on a scale of millions, the gas chambers, the cremation furnaces, the vile despoiling of corpses, all this was not supposed to be known, and in effect few did know it up to the end of the war. Among other precautions, in order to keep the secret, in official language only cautious and cynical euphemisms were employed: one did not write 'extermination' but 'final solution', not 'deportation' but 'transfer', not 'killing by gas' but 'special treatment', and so on. Not without reason, Hitler feared that this horrendous news, if it were divulged, would compromise the blind faith which the country had in him, as well as the morale of the fighting troops. Besides, it would have become known to the Allies and would have been exploited as propaganda material. This actually did happen, but because of their very enormity, the horrors of the camps, described many times by the Allied radio, were not generally believed.

The most convincing summing-up of the German situation at that time that I have found is in the book *Der SS Staat* (*The Theory and Practice of Hell*) by Eugene Kogon, a former Buchenwald prisoner, later Professor of Political Science at the University of Munich:

What did the Germans know about the concentration camps? Outside the concrete fact of their existence, almost nothing. Even today they know little. Indubitably, the method of rigorously keeping the details of the terrorist system secret, thereby making the anguish undefined, and hence that much more profound, proved very efficacious.

As I have said elsewhere, even many Gestapo functionaries did not know what was happening in the camps to which they were sending prisoners. The greater majority of the prisoners themselves had a very imprecise idea of how their camps functioned and of the methods employed there. How could the German people have known? Anyone who entered the camps found himself confronted by an unfathomable universe, totally new to him. This is the best demonstration of the power and efficacy of secrecy.

And yet . . . and yet, there wasn't even one German who did not know of the camps' existence or who believed they were sanatoriums. There were very few Germans who did not have a relative or an acquaintance in a camp, or who did not know, at least, that such a one or such another had been sent to a camp. All the Germans had been witnesses to the multiform anti-Semitic barbarity. Millions of them had been present – with indifference or with curiosity, with contempt or with downright malign joy – at the burning of synagogues or humiliation of Jews and Jewesses forced to kneel in the street mud. Many Germans knew from the foreign radio broadcasts, and a number had contact with prisoners who worked outside the camps. A good many Germans had had the experience of encountering miserable lines of prisoners in the streets or at the railroad stations. In a circular dated November 9, 1941, and addressed by the head of the Police and the Security Services to all . . . Police officials and camp commandants, one reads: 'In particular, it must be noted that during the transfers on foot, for example from the station to the camp, a considerable number of prisoners collapse along the way, fainting or dying from exhaustion . . . It is impossible to keep the population from knowing about such happenings.'

Not a single German could have been unaware of the fact that the prisons were full to overflowing, and that executions were taking place continually all over the country. Thousands of magistrates and police functionaries, lawyers, priests and social workers knew generically that the situation was very grave. Many businessmen who dealt with the camp SS men as suppliers, the industrialists who asked the administrative and economic offices of the SS for slave-laborers, the clerks in those offices, all knew perfectly well that many of the big firms were exploiting slave labor. Quite a few workers performed their tasks near concentration camps or actually inside them. Various university professors collaborated with the medical research centers instituted by Himmler, and various State doctors and doctors connected with private institutes collaborated with the professional murderers. A good many members of military aviation had been transferred to SS jurisdiction and must have known what went on there. Many high-ranking army officers knew about the mass murders of the Russian prisoners of war in the camps, and even more soldiers and members of the Military Police must have known exactly what terrifying horrors were being perpetrated in the camps, the ghettos, the cities, and the countrysides of the occupied Eastern territories. Can you say that even one of these statements is false?

In my opinion, none of these statements is false, but one other must be added to complete the picture: in spite of the varied possibilities for information, most Germans didn't know because they didn't want to know. Because, indeed, they wanted *not* to know. It is certainly true that State terrorism is a very strong weapon, very difficult to resist. But it is also true that the German people, as a whole, did not even try to resist. In Hitler's Germany a particular code was widespread: those who knew did not talk; those who did not know did not ask questions; those who did ask questions received no answers. In this way the typical German citizen won and defended his ignorance, which seemed to him sufficient justification for his adherence to Nazism. Shutting his mouth, his eyes and his ears, he built for himself the illusion of not knowing, hence not being an accomplice to the things taking place in front of his very door.

Knowing and making things known was one way (basically then not all that dangerous) of keeping one's distance from Nazism. I think the German people, on the whole, did not seek this recourse, and I hold them fully culpable of this deliberate omission.

3. Were there prisoners who escaped from the camps? How is it that there were no large-scale revolts?
These are among the questions most frequently put to me by young readers. They must, therefore, spring from some particularly important curiosity or need. My interpretation is optimistic: to-

day's young people feel that freedom is a privilege that one cannot do without, no matter what. Consequently, for them, the idea of prison is immediately linked to the idea of escape or revolt. Besides, it is true that according to the military codes of many countries, the prisoner of war is required to attempt escape, in any way possible, in order to resume his place as a combatant, and that according to The Hague Convention, such an attempt would not be punished. The concept of escape as a moral obligation is constantly reinforced by romantic literature (remember the Count of Monte Cristo?), by popular literature, and by the cinema, in which the hero, unjustly (or even justly) imprisoned, always tries to escape, even in the least likely circumstances, the attempt being invariably crowned with success.

Perhaps it is good that the prisoner's condition, not-liberty, is felt to be something improper, abnormal – like an illness, in short – that has to be cured by escape or rebellion. Unfortunately, however, this picture hardly resembles the true one of the concentration camps.

For instance, only a few hundred prisoners tried to escape from Auschwitz, and of those perhaps a few score succeeded. Escape was difficult and extremely dangerous. The prisoners were debilitated, in addition to being demoralised, by hunger and ill-treatment. Their heads were shaved, their striped clothing was immediately recognisable, and their wooden clogs made silent and rapid walking impossible. They had no money and, in general, did not speak Polish, which was the local language, nor did they have contacts in the area, the geography of which they did not know, either. On top of all that, fierce reprisals were employed to discourage escape attempts. Anyone caught trying to escape was publicly hanged – often after cruel torture – in the square where the roll-calls took place. When an escape was discovered, the friends of the fugitive were considered accomplices and were starved to death in cells; all the other prisoners were forced to remain standing for twenty-four hours, and sometimes the parents of the 'guilty' one were arrested and deported to camps.

The SS guards who killed a prisoner in the course of an escape attempt were granted special leaves. As a result, it often happened that an SS guard fired at a prisoner who had no intention of trying to escape, solely in order to qualify for leave. This fact artificially swells the official number of escape attempts recorded in the statistics. As I have indicated, the actual number was very small, made up almost exclusively of a few Aryan (that is, non-Jewish, to use the terminology of that time) Polish prisoners who lived not far from the camp and had, consequently, a goal toward which to proceed and the assurance that they would be protected by the population. In the other camps things occurred in a similar way.

As for the lack of rebellion, the story is somewhat different. First of all, it is necessary to remember that uprisings did actually take place in certain camps: Treblinka, Sobibor, even Birkenau, one of the Auschwitz dependencies. They did not have much numerical weight; like the analogous Warsaw Ghetto uprising, they represented, rather, examples of extraordinary moral force. In every instance they were planned and led by prisoners who were privileged in some way and, consequently, in better physical and spiritual condition than the average camp prisoner. This is not all that surprising: only at first glance does it seem paradoxical that people who rebel are those who suffer the least. Even outside the camps, struggles are rarely waged by *Lumpenproletariat*. People in rags do not revolt.

In the camps for political prisoners, or where political prisoners were in the majority, the conspiratorial experience of these people proved valuable and often resulted in quite effective defensive activities, rather than in open revolt. Depending upon the camps and the times, prisoners succeeded, for example, in blackmailing or corrupting the SS, curbing their indiscriminate power; in sabotaging the work for the German war industries; in organising escapes; in communicating via the radio with the Allies, furnishing them with accounts of the horrendous conditions in the camps; in improving the treatment of the sick, substituting prisoner doctors for the SS ones; in 'guiding' the selections, sending spies and traitors to death and saving prisoners whose survival had, for one reason or another, some special importance; preparing, even in military ways, to resist in case the Nazis decided (as in fact they often did decide), with the front coming closer, to liquidate the camps entirely.

In camps with a majority of Jews, like those in the Auschwitz area, an active or passive defence was particularly difficult. Here the prisoners were, for the most part, devoid of any kind of organisational or military experience. They came from every country in Europe, spoke different languages and, as a result, could not understand one another. They were more starved, weaker and more exhausted than the others because their living conditions were harsher and because they often had a long history of hunger, persecution and humiliation in the ghettos. The final consequence of this was that the length of their stays in the camps was tragically brief. They were, in short, a fluctuating population, continually decimated by death and renewed by the never-ending arrivals of new convoys. It is understandable that the seed of revolt did not easily take root in a human fabric that was in such a state of deterioration and so unstable.

You may wonder why the prisoners who had just got off the trains did not revolt, waiting as they did for hours (sometimes for days!) to enter the gas chambers. In addition to what I have already said, I must add here that the Germans had perfected a diabolically clever and versatile system of collective death. In most cases the new arrivals did not know what awaited them. They were received with cold efficiency but without brutality, invited to undress 'for the showers'. Sometimes they were handed soap and towels and were promised hot coffee after their showers. The gas chambers were, in fact, camouflaged as shower-rooms, with pipes, taps, dressing-rooms, clothes-hooks, benches and so forth. When, instead, prisoners showed the smallest sign of knowing or suspecting their imminent fate, the SS and their collaborators used surprise tactics, intervening with extreme brutality, with shouts, threats, kicks, shots, loosing their dogs, which were trained to tear prisoners to pieces, against people who were confused, desperate, weakened by five or ten days of travelling in sealed railroad cars.

Such being the case, the statement that has sometimes been formulated – that the Jews didn't revolt out of cowardice – appears absurd and insulting. No one rebelled. Let it suffice to remember that the gas chambers at Auschwitz were tested on a group of three hundred Russian prisoners of war, young, army-trained, politically indoctrinated, and not hampered by the presence of women and children, and even they did not revolt.

I would like to add one final thought. The deeply rooted consciousness that one must not consent to oppression but resist it instead was not widespread in Fascist Europe, and it was particularly weak in Italy. It was the patrimony of a narrow circle of political activists, but Fascism and Nazism had isolated, expelled, terrorised or destroyed them outright. You must not forget that the first victims of the German camps, by the hundreds of thousands, were, in fact, the cadres of the anti-Nazi political parties. Without their contribution, the popular will to resist, to organise for the purpose of resisting, sprang up again much later, thanks, above all, to the contribution of the European Communist parties that hurled themselves into the struggle against Nazism after Germany, in 1941, had unexpectedly attacked the Soviet Union, breaking the Ribbentrop–Molotov pact of September 1939. To conclude, reproaching the prisoners for not rebelling represents, above all, an error in historical perspective, expecting from them a political consciousness which is today an almost common heritage but which belonged at that time only to an elite.

4. Did you return to Auschwitz after the liberation?
I returned to Auschwitz twice, in 1965 and in 1982. As I have indicated in my books, the concentration-camp empire of Auschwitz did not consist of only one camp but rather of some forty camps. Auschwitz central was constructed on the outskirts of the town of the same name (Oswiecim, in Polish). It had a capacity of about 20,000 prisoners and was, so to speak, the administrative capital of the complex. Then there was the camp (or, to be more precise, the group of camps – from three to five, depending on the period) of Birkenau, which grew to contain about 60,000 prisoners, of whom about 40,000 were women, and in which the gas chambers and cremation furnaces functioned. In addition, there was a constantly varying number of work-camps, as far away as hundreds of kilometres from the 'capital'. My camp, called Monowitz, was the largest of these, containing, finally, about 12,000 prisoners. It was situated about seven kilometres to the east of Auschwitz. The whole area is now Polish territory.

I didn't feel anything much when I visited the central camp. The Polish government has transformed it into a kind of national monument. The huts have been cleaned and painted, trees have been planted and flower-beds laid out. There is a museum in which pitiful relics are displayed: tons of human hair, hundreds of thousands of eyeglasses, combs, shaving brushes, dolls, baby shoes, but it remains just a museum – something static, rearranged, contrived. To me, the entire camp seemed a museum. As for my own camp, it no longer exists. The rubber factory to which it was annexed, now in Polish hands, has grown so that it occupies the whole area.

I did, however, experience a feeling of violent anguish when I entered Birkenau camp, which I had never seen as a prisoner. Here nothing has changed. There was mud, and there is still mud, or suffocating summer dust. The blocks of huts (those that weren't burned when the front reached and passed this area) have remained as they were, low, dirty, with draughty wooden sides and beaten earth floors. There are no bunks but bare planks, all the way to the ceiling. Here nothing has been prettied up. With me was a woman friend of mine, Giuliana Tedeschi, a survivor of Birkenau. She pointed out to me that on every plank, 1.8 by 2 metres, up to nine women slept. She showed me that from the tiny window you could see the ruins of the cremation furnace. In her day, you could see the flames issuing from the chimney. She had asked the older women: 'What is that fire?' And they had replied: 'It is we who are burning.'

Face to face with the sad evocative power of those places, each of us survivors behaves in a different manner, but it is possible to describe two typical categories. Those who refuse to go back, or even to discuss the matter, belong to the first category, as do those who would like to forget but do not succeed in doing so and are tormented by nightmares and also another group who have, instead, forgotten, have dismissed everything, and have begun again to live, starting from zero. I have noticed that the first group are individuals who ended in the camps through bad luck, not because of a political commitment. For them the suffering was traumatic but devoid of meaning, like a misfortune or an illness. For them the memory is extraneous, a painful object which intruded into their lives and which they have sought – or still seek – to eliminate. The second category is composed, instead, of ex-political prisoners, or those who possessed at least a measure of political preparation, or religious conviction, or a strong moral consciousness. For these survivors, remembering is a duty. They do not want to forget, and above all they do not want the world to forget, because they understand that their experiences were not meaningless, that the camps were not an accident, an unforeseen historical happening.

The Nazi camps were the apex, the culmination of Fascism in Europe, its most monstrous manifestation, but Fascism existed before Hitler and Mussolini, and it survived, in open or masked forms, up to the defeat of World War II. In every part of the world, wherever you begin by denying the fundamental liberties of mankind, and equality among people, you move towards the concentration-camp system, and it is a road on which it is difficult to halt. I know many ex-prisoners who understand very well what a terrible lesson their experience contains and who return every year to 'their' camp, guiding pilgrimages of young people. I would do it myself, gladly, if time permitted, and if I did not know that I reached the same goal by writing books and by agreeing to talk about them to my readers.

5. Why do you speak only about German camps and not the Russian ones as well?

As I have already written in my reply to the first question, I prefer the role of witness to that of judge. I can bear witness only to the things which I myself endured and saw. My books are not history books. In writing them I have limited myself strictly to reporting facts of which I had direct experience, excluding those I learned later from books or newspapers. For example, you will note that I have not quoted the number of those massacred at Auschwitz, nor have I described details of the gas chambers and crematoria. This is because I did not, in fact, know these data when I was in the camp. I only learned them afterwards, when the whole world learned them.

For the same reason I do not generally speak about the Russian camps. Fortunately I was never in them, and I could repeat only the things I have read, which would be the same things known to everyone interested in the subject. Clearly, however, I do not want to, nor can I, evade the duty which every man has, that of making a judgement and formulating an opinion. Besides the obvious similarities, I think I can perceive substantial differences.

The principal difference lies in the finality. The German camps constitute something unique in the history of humanity, bloody as it is. To the ancient aim of eliminating or terrifying political adversaries, they set a monstrous modern goal, that of erasing entire peoples and cultures from the world. Starting roughly in 1941, they became gigantic death-machines. Gas chambers and crematoria were deliberately planned to destroy lives and human bodies on a scale of millions. The horrendous record belongs to Auschwitz, with 24,000 dead in a single day, in August 1944. Certainly the Soviet camps were not and are not pleasant places to be, but in them the death of prisoners was not expressly sought – even in the darkest years of Stalinism. It was a very frequent occurrence, tolerated with brutal indifference, but basically not intended. Death was a by-product of hunger, cold, infections, hard labour. In this lugubrious comparison between two models of hell, I must also add the fact that one entered the German camps, in general never to emerge. Death was the only foreseen outcome. In the Soviet camps, however, a possible limit to incarceration has always existed. In Stalin's day the 'guilty' were sometimes given terribly long sentences (as much as fifteen or twenty years) with frightening disregard, but a hope – however faint – of eventual freedom remained.

From this fundamental difference, the others arise. The relationships between guards and prisoners are less inhuman in the Soviet Union. They all belong to the same nation, speak the same language, are not labelled 'Supermen' and 'Non-men' as they were under Nazism. The sick are treated, though all too inadequately. Confronted with overly hard work, an individual or collective protest is not unthinkable. Corporal punishment is rare and not too cruel. It is possible to receive letters and packages with foodstuffs. Human personality, in short, is not denied and is not totally lost. As a general consequence, the mortality figures are very different under the two systems. In the Soviet Union, it seems that in the harshest periods mortality hovered around 30 per cent of those who entered. This is certainly an intolerably high figure, but in the German camps mortality mounted to between 90 and 98 per cent.

I find very serious the recent Soviet innovation, that of summarily declaring certain dissenting intellectuals insane, shutting them into psychiatric institutions, and subjecting them to treatments that not only cause cruel suffering but distort and weaken their mental functioning. This shows how greatly dissent is feared. It is no longer punished but there is an effort to destroy it with drugs (or with the threat of drugs). Perhaps this technique is not very widespread (it appears that in 1985 these political 'patients' do not exceed a hundred) but it is odious because it constitutes a despicable use of science and an unpardonable prostitution on the part of the doctors who lend themselves so slavishly to abetting the wishes of the authorities. It reveals extreme contempt for democratic confrontation and civil liberties.

On the other hand, and as far as the precisely quantitative aspect is concerned, one must note that in the Soviet Union the camp phenomenon appears to be on the decline, actually. It seems that around 1950, political prisoners were numbered in the millions. According to the data of Amnesty International they would number about ten thousand today.

To conclude, the Soviet camps remain anyway a deplorable manifestation of illegality and inhumanity. They have nothing to do with Socialism; indeed, they stand out as an ugly stain on Soviet Socialism. They should, rather, be regarded as a barbaric legacy from tsarist absolutism from which the Soviet rulers have been unable or have not wished to liberate themselves. Anyone who reads *Memories of a Dead House*, written by Dostoevsky in 1862, will have no difficulty recognising the same prison 'features' described by Solzhenitsyn a hundred years later. But it is possible, even easy, to picture a Socialism without prison camps. A Nazism without concentration camps is, instead, unimaginable.

6. Which of the characters in If This Is a Man *and* The Truce *have you seen again since the liberation?*
Most of the people who appear in these pages must, unfortunately, be considered to have died during their days in the camp or in the course of the huge evacuation march mentioned in the last chapter of the book. Others died later from illnesses contracted during their imprisonment. I have been unable to find a trace of still others. Some few survive and I have been able to maintain or re-establish contact with them.

Jean, the 'Pikolo' of 'The Canto of Ulysses', is alive and well. His family had been wiped out, but he married after his return and now has two children and leads a very peaceful life as a pharmacist in a small town in the French provinces. We get together occasionally in Italy, where he holidays. At other times I have gone to join him. Strange as it may seem, he has forgotten much of his year in Monowitz. The atrocious memories of the evacuation march loom larger for him. In the course of it, he saw all his friends (Alberto among them) die of exhaustion.

I also quite often see the person I called Piero Sonnino (the man who appears as Cesare in *The Truce*). He too, after a difficult period of 're-entry,' found work and built a family. He lives in Rome. He recounts willingly and with great liveliness the vicissitudes he lived through in camp and during the long journey home, but in his narratives, which often become almost theatrical monologues, he tends to emphasise the adventurous happenings of which he was the protagonist rather than those tragic ones at which he was passively present.

I have also seen Charles again. He had been taken prisoner only in November 1944 in the hills of the Vosges near his house, where he was a partisan, and he had been in the camp for only a month. But that month of suffering, and the terrible things which he witnessed, marked him deeply, robbing him of the joy of living and the desire to build a future. Repatriated after a journey much like the one I described in *The Truce*, he resumed his profession of elementary school teacher in the tiny school in his village, where he also taught the children how to raise bees and how to cultivate a nursery for firs and pine trees. He retired quite a few years ago and recently married a no-longer-young colleague. Together they built a new house, small but comfortable and charming. I have gone to visit him twice, in 1951 and 1974. On this last occasion he told me about Arthur, who lives in a village not far from him. Arthur is old and ill, and does not wish to receive visits that might reawaken old anguish.

Dramatic, unforeseen, and full of joy for both of us was rediscovering Mendi, the 'modernist rabbi' mentioned briefly. He recognised himself in 1965 while casually reading the German translation of *If This Is a Man*, remembered me, and wrote me a long letter, addressing it care of the Jewish Community of Turin. We subsequently wrote to each other at length, each informing the other about the fates of our common friends. In 1967 I went to see him in Dortmund, in the German Republic, where he was rabbi at the time. He has remained as he was, 'steadfast, courageous, and keen', and extraordinarily cultivated besides. He married an Auschwitz survivor and has three children, now grown-up. The whole family intends to move to Israel.

I never saw Dr Pannwitz again. He was the chemist who subjected me to a chilling 'State examination'. But I heard about him from that Dr Müller to whom I dedicated the chapter 'Vanadium' in my book *The Periodic Table*. When the arrival of the Red Army at the Buna factory was imminent, he conducted himself like a bully and a coward. He ordered his civilian collaborators to resist to the bitter end, forbade them to climb aboard the train leaving for the zones behind the front, but jumped on himself at the last moment, profiting from the confusion. He died in 1946 of a brain tumour.

I have lost contact with almost all the characters in *The Truce*, with the exception of Cesare (of whom I have spoken before) and Leonardo. Dr Leonardo De Benedetti, a native of Turin like myself, had lost his dearly beloved wife at Auschwitz. After returning to our city, he resumed his profession with courage and commitment and was a precious friend, wise and serene, for many years. Besides his patients, innumerable others turned to him for help and advice and were never disappointed. He died in 1983 at the age of eighty-five, without suffering.

7. How can the Nazis' fanatical hatred of the Jews be explained?
It can be said that anti-Semitism is one particular case of intoler-

ance; that for centuries it had a prevailingly religious character; that in the Third Reich it was exacerbated by the nationalistic and military predisposition of the German people and by the 'differentness' of the Jewish people; that it was easily disseminated in all of Germany – and in a good part of Europe – thanks to the efficiency of the Fascist and Nazi propaganda which needed a scapegoat on which to load all guilts and all resentments; and that the phenomenon was heightened to paroxysm by Hitler, a maniacal dictator.

However, I must admit that these commonly accepted explanations do not satisfy me. They are reductive; not commensurate with, nor proportionate to, the facts that need explaining. In rereading the chronicles of Nazism, from its murky beginnings to its convulsed end, I cannot avoid the impression of a general atmosphere of uncontrolled madness that seems to me to be unique in history. This collective madness, this 'running off the rails', is usually explained by postulating the combination of many diverse factors, insufficient if considered singly, and the greatest of these factors is Hitler's personality itself and its profound interaction with the German people. It is certain that his personal obsessions, his capacity for hatred, his preaching of violence, found unbridled echoes in the frustration of the German people, and for this reason came back to him multiplied, confirming his delirious conviction that he himself was the Hero prophesied by Nietzsche, the Superman redeemer of Germany.

Much has been written about the origin of his hatred of the Jews. It is said that Hitler poured out upon the Jews his hatred of the entire human race; that he recognised in the Jews some of his own defects, and that in hating the Jews he was hating himself; that the violence of his aversion arose from the fear that he might have 'Jewish blood' in his veins.

Again, these explanations do not seem adequate to me. I do not find it permissible to explain a historical phenomenon by piling all the blame on a single individual (those who carry out horrendous orders are not innocent!). Besides, it is always difficult to interpret the deep-seated motivations of an individual. The hypotheses that have been proposed justify the facts only up to a point, explain the quality but not the quantity. I must admit that I prefer the humility with which some of the most serious historians (among them Bullock, Schramm, Bracher) confess to *not understanding* the furious anti-Semitism of Hitler and of Germany behind him.

Perhaps one cannot, what is more one must not, understand what happened, because to understand is almost to justify. Let me explain: 'understanding' a proposal or human behaviour means to 'contain' it, contain its author, put oneself in his place, identify with him. Now, no normal human being will ever be able to identify with Hitler, Himmler, Goebbels, Eichmann, and endless others. This dismays us, and at the same time gives us a sense of relief, because perhaps it is desirable that their words (and also, unfortunately, their deeds) cannot be comprehensible to us. They are non-human words and deeds, really counter-human, without historic precedents, with difficulty comparable to the cruellest events of the biological struggle for existence. The war can be related to this struggle, but Auschwitz has nothing to do with war; it is neither an episode in it nor an extreme form of it. War is always a terrible fact, to be deprecated, but it is in us, it has its rationality, we 'understand' it.

But there is no rationality in the Nazi hatred: it is a hate that is not in us; it is outside man, it is a poison fruit sprung from the deadly trunk of Fascism, but it is outside and beyond Fascism itself. We cannot understand it, but we can and must understand from whence it springs, and we must be on our guard. If understanding is impossible, knowing is imperative, because what happened could happen again. Conscience can be seduced and obscured again – even our consciences.

For this reason, it is everyone's duty to reflect on what happened. Everybody must know, or remember, that when Hitler and Mussolini spoke in public, they were believed, applauded, admired, adored like gods. They were 'charismatic leaders'; they possessed a secret power of seduction that did not proceed from the credibility or the soundness of the things they said but from the suggestive way in which they said them, from their eloquence, from their histrionic art, perhaps instinctive, perhaps patiently learnt and practised. The ideas they proclaimed were not always the same and were, in general, aberrant or silly or cruel. And yet they were acclaimed with hosannahs and followed to the death by millions of the faithful. We must remember that these faithful followers, among them the diligent executors of inhuman orders, were not born torturers, were not (with a few exceptions) monsters: they were ordinary men. Monsters exist, but they are too few in number to be truly dangerous. More dangerous are the common men, the functionaries ready to believe and to act without asking questions, like Eichmann; like Hoss, the commandant of Auschwitz; like Stangl, commandant of Treblinka; like the French military of twenty years later, slaughterers in Algeria; like the Khmer Rouge of the late seventies, slaughterers in Cambodia.

It is, therefore, necessary to be suspicious of those who seek to convince us with means other than reason, and of charismatic leaders: we must be cautious about delegating to others our judgement and our will. Since it is difficult to distinguish true prophets from false, it is as well to regard all prophets with suspicion. It is better to renounce revealed truths, even if they exalt us by their splendour or if we find them convenient because we can acquire them gratis. It is better to content oneself with other more modest and less exciting truths, those one acquires painfully, little by little and without short cuts, with study, discussion, and reasoning, those that can be verified and demonstrated.

It is clear that this formula is too simple to suffice in every case. A new Fascism, with its trail of intolerance, of abuse, and of servitude, can be born outside our country and be imported into it, walking on tiptoe and calling itself by other names, or it can loose itself from within with such violence that it routs all defences. At that point, wise counsel no longer serves, and one must find the strength to resist. Even in this contingency, the memory of what happened in the heart of Europe, not very long ago, can serve as support and warning.

8. What would you be today if you had not been a prisoner in the camp? What do you feel, remembering that period? To what factors do you attribute your survival?

Strictly speaking, I do not and cannot know what I would be today if I had not been in the camp. No man knows his future, and this would be, precisely, a case of describing a future that never took place. Hazarding guesses (extremely rough ones, for that matter) about the behaviour of a population has some meaning. It is, however, almost impossible to foresee the behaviour of an individual, even on a day-to-day basis. In the same way, the physicist can prognosticate with great exactitude the time a gram of radium will need to halve its activity, but is totally unable to say when a single atom of that same radium will disintegrate. If a man sets out towards a crossroad and does not take the left hand path, it is obvious that he will take the one on the right, but almost never are our choices between only two alternatives. Then, every choice is followed by others, all multiple, and so on, *ad infinitum.* Last of all, our future depends heavily on external factors, wholly extraneous to our deliberate choices, and on internal factors as well, of which we are, however, not aware. For these well-known reasons, one does not know one's future or that of one's neighbour. For the same reason no one can say what his past would have been like 'if'.

I can, however, formulate a certain assertion and it is this: if I had not lived the Auschwitz experience, I probably would never have written anything. I would not have had the motivation, the incentive, to write. I had been a mediocre student in Italian and had had bad grades in history. Physics and chemistry interested me most, and I had chosen a profession, that of chemist, which had nothing in common with the world of the written word. It was the experience of the camp and the long journey home that forced me to write. I did not have to struggle with laziness, problems of style seemed ridiculous to me, and miraculously I found the time to write without taking even one hour away from my daily professional work. It seemed as if those books were all there, ready in my head, and I had only to let them come out and pour on to paper.

Now many years have passed. The two books, above all the first, have had many adventures and have interposed themselves, in a curious way, like an artificial memory, but also like a defensive barrier, between my very normal present and the dramatic past. I say this with some hesitation, because I would not want to pass for a cynic: when I remember the camp today, I no longer feel any violent or dolorous emotions. On the contrary, on to my brief and tragic experience as a deportee has been overlaid that much longer and complex experience of writer-witness, and the sum total is clearly positive: in its totality, this past has made me richer and surer. A friend of mine, who was deported to the women's camp of Ravensbrück, says that the camp was her university. I think I can say the same thing, that is, by living and then writing about and pondering those events, I have learned many things about man and about the world.

I must hasten to say, however, that this positive outcome was a kind of good fortune granted to very few. Of the Italian deportees, for example, only about five per cent returned, and many of these lost families, friends, property, health, equilibrium, youth. The fact that I survived and returned unharmed is due, in my opinion, chiefly to good luck. Pre-existing factors played only a small part: for instance, my training as a mountaineer and my profession of chemist, which won me some privileges in the last months of imprisonment. Perhaps I was helped too by my interest, which has never flagged, in the human spirit and by the will not only to survive (which was common to many) but to survive with the precise purpose of recounting the things we had witnessed and endured. And, finally, I was also helped by the determination, which I stubbornly preserved, to recognise always, even in the darkest days, in my companions and in myself, men, not things, and thus to avoid that total humiliation and demoralisation which led so many to spiritual shipwreck.

PRIMO LEVI
TRANSLATED BY RUTH FELDMAN